ARTICLE 9 PLAINLY STATED

ADRIAN COHEN
Adjunct Professor,
University of Wisconsin Law School and
Arizona State University Sandra Day O'Connor College of Law

LAURA N. COORDES
Associate Professor of Law,
Arizona State University Sandra Day O'Connor College of Law

860 Blue Gentian Road, Suite 350
Eagan, MN 55121
1-877-888-1330

Printed in the United States of America

ISBN: 978-1-68561-439-3

WEST ACADEMIC PUBLISHING'S EMERITUS ADVISORY BOARD

WEST ACADEMIC PUBLISHING'S LAW SCHOOL ADVISORY BOARD

To Carla, Adam, Michaela, Laura, Tom & Charlie
for patient support through the years,
To Prof. Gerald J. Thain, mentor on all things
Article Nine. . .and baseball, and
To Brendan Wolf for bringing the draft to the digital age

A.C.

To Greg, Calliope, and Aurelia, for all you are and all you do

L.N.C.

To our students, who test drove the concept of this book over the years.

INTRODUCTION

As professors who have collectively taught Article Nine of the Uniform Commercial Code ("UCC") to thousands of students over a combined 47 years, the most common complaint we hear from our students is, "Why was it written that way? I can't understand this!" We even hear this from practitioners who have to tackle the subject from time to time.

This book seeks to address that complaint directly. In it, we provide you with a direct reference to each provision of Article Nine of the UCC, written in plain, easy-to-understand language. You'll also find examples, tips, and even a visual aid or two to help you make sense of this statute, which can at times be complex and unruly.

This book is designed to be read in conjunction with Article Nine. By tracking the statutory provisions, we give you, our readers, the tools you need to understand and apply the statute. Every provision of Article Nine is reproduced below, but in a plainer format designed to help you understand what the provision means and how it fits into the larger scheme of Article Nine. Instead of learning concepts divorced from the statute, this book allows you to work closely with the statute so that you can gain a better understanding of how to read and interpret the UCC. Thus, although it is unlikely that you will read this book cover-to-cover, you can and should use it as a reference book for better understanding Article Nine, and you should read it alongside any Article Nine provisions you encounter.

We hope this book will be a useful resource for anyone who encounters Article Nine in some way. Good luck on your journey through this complex yet fascinating statute!

TABLE OF CONTENTS

INTRODUCTION v

Introduction to the 9–100s 1
9–101: What to Call Article Nine 2
9–102: Definitions 3
9–103: Purchase-Money Security Interests 21
9–104: When a Secured Party Has "Control" over a Deposit Account 23
9–105: When a Secured Party Has "Control" over Electronic Chattel Paper 24
9–106: When a Person Has "Control" over Investment Property 25
9–107: When a Secured Party Has "Control" over a Letter of Credit Right 26
9–108: How to Describe Collateral 27
9–109: The Scope of Article Nine 28
9–110: Security Interests Involving Articles 2 and 2A 31
Introduction to the 9–200s 32
9–201: The Security Agreement's Effectiveness 33
9–202: "Title" Doesn't Matter 34
9–203: Requirements for Attachment 35
9–204: Attachment of After-Acquired Collateral 37
9–205: The Security Interest Is Still Attached in These Situations 38
9–206: Security Interests in Certain Financial Assets 39
9–207: Secured Party's Treatment of Collateral in Its Possession or Control 40
9–208: How a Secured Party Relinquishes Control in Certain Property Once Paid 41
9–209: Once Paid, a Secured Party Should Notify Account Debtors Not to Pay Them 43
9–210: How a Debtor Gets Information from a Secured Party About Certain Collateral 44
Introduction to the 9–300s 45
9–301: What Law Governs Perfection and Priority for Security Interests 46
9–302: What Law Governs Perfection and Priority for Agricultural Liens 48
9–303: What Law Governs Perfection and Priority for Goods Covered by a Certificate of Title 49
9–304: What Law Governs Perfection and Priority for Deposit Accounts 50
9–305: What Law Governs Perfection and Priority for Investment Property 51
9–306: What Law Governs Perfection and Priority for Letter-of-Credit Rights 52
9–307: How to Determine the Debtor's Location 53
9–308: When a Security Interest or Agricultural Lien Is Perfected 54
9–309: Automatic Perfection 55

9–310: When a Secured Party Must File a Financing Statement to Perfect 56
9–311: When Special Laws Apply to Perfection 57
9–312: Perfection (Including Temporary Perfection) of Security Interests in Chattel Paper, Negotiable Documents, Instruments, Investment Property, Deposit Accounts, Letter-of-Credit Rights, and Money 58
9–313: Perfection by Possession or Delivery 60
9–314: Perfection by Control 61
9–315: What Happens upon Disposition of Collateral 62
9–316: What Happens When the Governing Law Changes 64
9–317: Priority of Security Interest and Agricultural Lien v. Another Interest 66
9–318: What Happens When the Debtor Sells an Account, Chattel Paper, Payment Intangible or Promissory Note 67
9–319: A Consignee's Rights and Title v. Those of Other Parties 68
9–320: When Buyers of Goods Take Free of Security Interests 69
9–321: Licensees and Lessees in the Ordinary Course of Business 70
9–322: Priority of Competing Security Interests and Agricultural Liens 71
9–323: Priority with Respect to Future Advances 73
9–324: Special Priority for Purchase-Money Security Interests 75
9–325: Priority in Transferred Collateral 77
9–326: Priority of Security Interests Created in a New Debtor's Property 78
9–327: Priority of Security Interests in Deposit Accounts 79
9–328: Priority of Security Interests in Investment Property 80
9–329: Priority of Security Interests in Letter-of-Credit Rights 81
9–330: Priority of Purchasers of Chattel Paper or Instruments 82
9–331: Limitations of Article Nine with Respect to Negotiable Instruments, Negotiable Documents, and Investment Securities 83
9–332: Transfer of Money or Funds from a Deposit Account 84
9–333: Priority of Possessory Liens 85
9–334: Fixtures 86
9–335: Security Interests in Accessions 88
9–336: Security Interests in Commingled Goods 89
9–337: Priority in Goods Covered by a Certificate of Title 90
9–338: What Happens if a Security Interest or Agricultural Lien Is Perfected by a Filing that Provides Incorrect Information 91
9–339: Priority Can Be Voluntarily Subordinated 92
9–340: Bank's Set-Off or Recoupment Rights 93
9–341: Bank's Rights and Duties Regarding a Deposit Account 94
9–342: Bank's Rights with Respect to a Control Agreement 95
Introduction to the 9–400s 96
9–401: A Debtor's Ability to Transfer Rights in Collateral 97
9–402: Secured Party's Liability for Debtor's Actions 98
9–403: Agreement Between Account Debtor and Assignor 99

9–404: Assignee's Rights and Limitations 100
9–405: Modification of an Assigned Contract 101
9–406: Assignments and Account Debtors 102
9–407: Restrictions Regarding Leases of Goods 104
9–408: Ineffective Restrictions on Certain Assignments 105
9–409: Ineffective Restrictions on Assignment of Letter-of-Credit Rights 107
Introduction to the 9–500s 108
9–501: The Filing Office 109
9–502: What to Include in a Financing Statement 110
9–503 Alt A: How to Identify the Debtor and the Secured Party 111
9–503 Alt B: How to Identify the Debtor and the Secured Party 113
9–504: How to Describe Collateral in a Financing Statement 116
9–505: Special Financing Statement Rules for Consignments, Leases, Bailments, and Certain Other Transactions 117
9–506: What Errors Make a Financing Statement Seriously Misleading 118
9–507: Effectiveness of a Financing Statement in Light of Changes 119
9–508: What Happens to the Financing Statement When a "New Debtor" Comes into the Picture 120
9–509: Who Can File 121
9–510: Authorization and Effectiveness of Financing Statements 122
9–511: The Secured Party of Record 123
9–512 Alt A: Amending a Financing Statement 124
9–512 Alt B: Amending a Financing Statement 125
9–513: Filing a Termination Statement 126
9–514: When the Secured Party Assigns Its Power to Authorize Amendments 127
9–515: When a Financing Statement Lapses, and How to File a Continuation Statement 128
9–516: When "Filing" Occurs (and Doesn't) 129
9–517: When the Filing Office Makes a Mistake 131
9–518 Alt A: Filing an Information Statement 132
9–518 Alt B: Filing an Information Statement 133
9–519 Alt A: How to Index and Communicate Information on Records 135
9–519 Alt B: How to Index and Communicate Information on Records 137
9–520: Filing Office's Refusal to File a Record 139
9–521: Form of Financing Statement 140
9–522 Alt A: Keeping and Destroying Financing Statements 141
9–522 Alt B: Keeping and Destroying Financing Statements 142
9–523: Information from the Filing Office 143
9–524: When Filing Office Is Excused 144
9–525: Filing Fees 145
9–526: Filing Office Rules 146
9–527: Report on the Filing Office's Operations 147

TABLE OF CONTENTS

Introduction to the 9–600s 148
9–601: Rights After Default 149
9–602: Rules that Cannot Be Waived or Varied 150
9–603: Parties' Agreement on Standards 151
9–604: The Secured Party's Options if the Security Agreement Covers Real Property or Fixtures 152
9–605: Limitation of Secured Party's Duties 153
9–606: When a Default Occurs on an Agricultural Lien 154
9–607: Secured Party's Options for Collection and Enforcement of Rights 155
9–608: Application of Proceeds Generated from Collection or Enforcement 156
9–609: Post-Default Repossession Rights 157
9–610: Disposition of Collateral 158
9–611: Notification of Disposition 159
9–612: When a Notification Is Sent Within a Reasonable Time 160
9–613: Contents of the Notification 161
9–614: Contents of the Notification for Consumer-Goods Transactions 162
9–615: How to Apply Proceeds Generated by a Disposition 163
9–616: Explaining How a Surplus or Deficiency is Calculated 165
9–617: Transferee's Rights 167
9–618: Secondary Obligors' Rights and Obligations 168
9–619: Transfer Statements 169
9–620: Strict Foreclosure 170
9–621: Notification of Strict Foreclosure 172
9–622: Effect of Strict Foreclosure 173
9–623: Redemption of Collateral 174
9–624: What Can Be Waived 175
9–625: When the Secured Party Fails to Comply 176
9–626: Rules if an Issue About Deficiency or Surplus Exists 177
9–627: When Is Conduct Commercially Reasonable? 178
9–628: Limitations on Secured Party's Liability 179

ARTICLE 9
PLAINLY STATED

INTRODUCTION TO THE 9–100s

The 9–100s (also sometimes known as "Part 1" of Article Nine) are the general provisions of Article Nine. Here you'll find some "housekeeping" items, like definitions (9–102) and the scope of Article Nine (9–109). The 9–100s also cover some general concepts, like a purchase-money security interest (9–103), what it means to have "control" of certain collateral (9–104 through 9–107), and how a secured party should describe collateral (9–108). Overall, this is the section where you'd look to figure out what Article Nine covers, and what the terminology used throughout Article Nine means.

9–101: WHAT TO CALL ARTICLE NINE

If you want to call this Article something, call it the "Uniform Commercial Code-Secured Transactions."

9–102: DEFINITIONS

9–102(a)(1)

An "**accession**" is a good that is stuck together with another good in a way that allows you to see that both goods still exist separately from each other.

Note: A "good" is something physical and moveable. See 9–102(a)(44).

Example: A tractor, which is a good, has a new engine, also a good, installed; the engine is an accession to the tractor, and the tractor is an accession to the engine.

9–102(a)(2)

"Account" covers lots of things when it's used to describe a type of collateral, as opposed to being used to say something like one party must "account for" some item to another party. Some of the things that Article Nine calls "accounts" may seem a lot like things that are not accounts (for instance, see "payment intangible" in 9–102(a)(61)), so pay attention here.

An account is a right to get paid in money, even if you haven't done anything yet to fully earn the right to actually get the payment, for the following things:

(i) property that you sold or you're going to sell to someone who's promised to buy; and property that you've leased or are going to lease to someone who's promised to lease it from you; and property that you've licensed or are going to license (usually, this property has an intellectual property component of some kind, like copyrights); and property you've assigned or you're going to assign to someone; and property that you disposed of in some way that doesn't fall under the categories just listed.

It is pretty hard to imagine something falling into that last category, but it gets the point across that "accounts" has a broad meaning when it comes to property you're somehow transferring to someone else, where that somebody still owes you payment.

We're nowhere near done yet, because now we move to (ii) and beyond, using the same preamble clause to (i) (that is, "An account is a right to get paid in money. . .")

(ii) for services you rendered or plan to render;

Example: You provided your services as an attorney. Now your client owes you for your time spent.

Example: You commit yourself to provide your legal services in return for a retainer that your client owes upfront. Even if you haven't done a lick of work yet, this is an account.

(iii) for an insurance policy that was issued or is going to be issued;

(iv) for a promise or guarantee to pay what someone else owes if they don't pay;

Example: A co-signor's obligation to pay is an "account" because it's a distinct secondary obligation. For more detail, see 9–102(a)(72).

(v) for energy that has been provided or is going to be provided;

(vi) for using a vessel like a ship or boat or intergalactic transporter that has been chartered or otherwise hired;

(vii) for anything purchased or owed because of the use of a credit or charge card or anything encoded on or just plain required for payment due to the use of the card;

Note: This includes the charge card company's right to receive payment from its cardholder, and not just the retailer's right to get paid for merchandise it sold.

(viii) for hitting it big (or small) in legal gambling, like a lottery, that is authorized by States or their governmental units.

Just to confuse everybody, part of the definition of "accounts" isn't even numbered, and some of it is duplicate-numbered. The rest of what follows is that part:

"Accounts" also include "health care receivables," which 9–102(a)(46) tells us is the right to be paid under insurance for providing health goods or services.

Here's what we're excluding from the definition of "account":

(i) a right to get paid that is evidenced by chattel paper (see 9–102(a)(11)) or an instrument (like a promissory note, bank check or other thing described in 9–102(a)(47));

(ii) commercial tort claims;

Example: A claim for tortious interference with an employment contract may create a right to payment, but that is handled separately under other law and is further dealt with in 9–109(d) and 9–401.

(iii) bank accounts and similar types of deposit accounts;

Note: These are still covered as a type of Article Nine collateral. . .just not as "accounts."

(iv) "investment property" (see 9–102(a)(49));

(v) letter-of-credit-rights or letters-of-credit (see 9–102(a)(51)); or

Note: These are dealt with in 9–329 but are more fully covered by Article Five. Because they sound like they'd fit under our definition of "account," we make a point of breaking them out from the overall definition.

(vi) rights to payment for loans or other advances of money, which has implications for understanding the separate handling of "payment intangibles."

Note: Rights to credit or charge card payments *are* included in our definition of "account." See 9–102(a)(2)(vii).

Note: If something that someone owes isn't an "account," then it's probably a special kind of general intangible called a "payment intangible." See 9–102(a)(61).

9–102(a)(3)

An "**account debtor**" is a person that is obligated to pay on an account, chattel paper or general intangible.

Note: "Person" is defined in 1–201(b)(27).

Note: An account debtor is *not* a person that is responsible to pay on a negotiable instrument, like a bank check or a negotiable promissory note. This is true even if the instrument is part of "chattel paper." There are separate rules for that situation.

Example: A dentist filled a patient's cavity, with payment due in 60 days. This transaction created an account (see 9–102(a)(2)), and the patient, who is obligated to pay on the account, is the account debtor.

9–102(a)(4)

"**Accounting**," except when we use it generically as in "accounting for," means a record with three features:

(A) It is authenticated by the secured party.

(B) It shows the unpaid amount of a secured debt obligation in one of two ways:

It shows the amount that is still unpaid 35 days or less before the record was made; or

It shows the amount that will be owed 35 days or less after the record was made.

(C) It identifies in some reasonable level of detail what it is that makes up the obligation

Note: A "reasonable level of detail" would be something like a breakout of interest, principal, late fees, and so on.

9–102(a)(5)

"**Agricultural lien**" means an interest in farm products with three distinct features:

(A) It serves as security or "for" amounts owed for goods or services or rent or lease of real estate that were provided in connection with a debtor's farm operations;

(B) A statute says that it creates a lien in favor of a person who:

(i) as part of the ordinary course of business provided goods or services so a debtor could use them for the debtor's farming operations, or

(ii) leased real estate to a debtor so the debtor could use it as part of the debtor's farming operations

(C) It doesn't require the secured party to possess the debtor's farm products.

Example: A farm supply store sells seeds to a farmer on credit. In the state where the farmer's farm is located, a statute creates a lien in favor of the farm supply store on the seeds and any crops grown from the seeds. This lien is an agricultural lien.

9–102(a)(6)

"**As extracted collateral**" has two possible meanings:

(A) oil, gas or other extracted minerals that are included in a security interest that

(i) is created by a debtor who has an interest in the minerals before they're extracted and

(ii) attaches to the minerals in whatever form they're in once extracted; or

(B) accounts that come into being from a sale that takes place at the point where the minerals emerge at the wellhead or minehead where the debtor had an interest in them before they were extracted.

9–102(a)(7)

"**Authenticate**" means to

(A) physically sign; or

(B) place a symbol or encrypt or otherwise process it into a computerized record to show a person's intent to identify who they are and to say they adopt or accept the record.

Example: A person signs a document simply using the letter "X." That person has authenticated the document. "X" serves as a substitute for a signature. It identifies the person and indicates their intent to accept or adopt the record.

9–102(a)(8)

"**Bank**" means a bank. This includes a credit union, savings and loan or whatever institution provides the kinds of services a "bank" provides.

9–102(a)(9)

"**Cash proceeds**" means things like money (cash), bank checks, or funds deposited in bank accounts ("deposit accounts") that are received from the sale of property that served as collateral.

9–102(a)(10)

"**Certificate of title**" means a certificate that, under the law of the jurisdiction that issues the certificate, requires that a secured party have its security interest listed on the certificate if it wants to perfect in a way that would give it superior rights compared to a "lien creditor." "Certificate of title" also describes other records on which the jurisdiction may permit or require the secured party's notation of its interest if it wants to have a claim that beats a lien creditor's claim.

9–102(a)(11)

"**Chattel paper**" is a name we made up to describe something that existed but didn't have a simple name. It boils down to this: Chattel paper is a record of some kind that shows that both a money interest is owed and that there is a security interest in specific goods that backs up the money interest that's owed.

Note: A *lease* of specific goods is chattel paper because a lease is a kind of monetary obligation that allows repossession if the lease payments aren't made.

Example: A promissory note stapled to a security agreement that itself backs up payment of the promissory note. The two documents together are "chattel paper" because they show that a money interest is owed (thanks to the promissory note) and that there is a security interest (thanks to the security agreement).

But there's so much more. We also use the term "chattel paper" to describe the monetary obligation in certain software arrangements, so a security interest may be not just in specific goods but also in the software used in the goods. Think of a program in a computer: the computer is the goods, the program is the software. This is so even if the software is licensed rather than sold outright—so the license may be treated as property that serves as security. If you don't pay up on the goods or the license, the creditor can void (take back) the license to use the software. And, to be consistent with a *lease* serving as chattel paper, we see that the lease of specific goods and a license of software in the goods is also chattel paper.

For purposes of the definition of "chattel paper," a "monetary obligation" means a debt that the secured goods cover or what's owed under a lease, and the term also includes whatever is owed for software used in the goods.

The term "chattel paper" doesn't include the following things that might look like our definition of chattel paper but don't fit into what we're trying to accomplish here:

(i) charters or other nautical contracts for hiring a boat or airship; and

(ii) credit card-related transactions

Both of these situations are covered via an "account," defined in 9–102(a)(2).

If one or more *instruments* (e.g. promissory notes) are part of a transaction or a series of transactions that include records other than the instruments, then all the records together are chattel paper. In other words, the records don't each have to be matched up to a single, separate instrument or security agreement.

9–102(a)(12)

"**Collateral**" means the personal and other property that is the subject of a security interest or agricultural lien. It includes all of the following:

(A) "proceeds" from the disposition of the property if the security interest attaches to those proceeds

(B) accounts, chattel paper, general intangibles and promissory notes that have been *sold* as opposed to used as collateral in the usual way in connection with an extension of credit or other obligation

(C) goods that are held on "consignment," as that term is used in its specialized way in 9–102(a)(20).

Note: Recall that 9–109(a)(3) says the kinds of *sales* transactions in (B) fall under Article Nine even if they have no credit aspect to them.

9–102(a)(13)

A "**commercial tort claim**" is one in which

(A) the claimant is an organization, not an individual, or

(B) the claimant is an individual who is suing over a claim that came about in the individual's business or profession if that claim in either situation isn't seeking damages for personal injury or wrongful death.

9–102(a)(14)

A "**commodity account**" is an account in which a commodity intermediary, like a broker, maintains a customer's commodity contract on the intermediary's own record.

9–102(a)(15)

A "**commodity contract**" is a futures contract or an option on a futures or regular contract if the contract or option is traded on or subject to:

(A) a board of trade regulated under federal commodities law, or

(B) a foreign board of trade exchange or market,

and in either situation is carried on the books of a commercial intermediary for the customer.

9–102(a)(16)

A "**commodity customer**" is the person for whom the commodity intermediary (e.g., broker) is holding the commodity contract on its books.

9–102(a)(17)

A "**commodity intermediary**" is a person that:

(A) is registered under federal law to trade futures on commission, or

(B) is a clearinghouse for commodities transactions for a federally-designated board of trade.

9–102(a)(18)

"**Communicate**" means:

(A) to send a written or other physical record;

(B) to transmit a record in a way the sending and receiving parties have agreed to; or

(C) to follow a filing office's rules for transmitting records.

9–102(a)(19)

A "**consignee**" is a merchant that receives goods it will sell on "consignment," as defined in 9–102(a)(20).

9–102(a)(20)

There is consignment law that governs consignments outside of Article Nine. However, Article Nine does govern some kinds of consignments. You're dealing with an Article Nine "**consignment"** rather than a "true consignment" (i.e., one that's governed by law outside of Article Nine) if the answer is "yes" to all the questions in the *lefthand* column below, and "no" to all of the questions in the *righthand* column.

Are the goods (tangible things) delivered to the "consignee" (defined in 9–102(a)(19)) for the purpose of sale?	Is the consignee an auctioneer?
Is the consignee a merchant?	Do the consignee's creditors generally know that the consignee is substantially in the business of selling other people's goods?
Does the consignee sell goods like these?	Are the goods the consignor's "consumer goods"?
Is the consignee's name different from the consignor's?	Are the goods delivered as part of a security agreement between the consignor and consignee?
Are the goods altogether worth $1,000 or more?	
If all the above answers are YES...	**...and all the above answers are NO...**

...then you have an Article 9 consignment!

9–102(a)(21)

A "**consignor**" is a person who delivers goods to a merchant so the merchant will hopefully sell them for that person.

9–102(a)(22)

A "**consumer debtor**" is a debtor in a consumer transaction.

9–102(a)(23)

"**Consumer goods**" are goods used or bought primarily to use for personal, family or household purposes.

9–102(a)(24)

A "**consumer goods transaction**" is a consumer transaction where an individual takes on an obligation primarily for personal, family or household purposes—in other words, not for business purposes—and consumer goods are the collateral that secures payment of the obligation.

9–102(a)(25)

A "**consumer obligor**" is an individual who takes on an obligation as part of a transaction that primarily is for personal, family or household purposes.

9–102(a)(26)

A "**consumer transaction**" is a transaction where an individual takes on an obligation primarily for personal, family or household purposes and uses collateral that is primarily for personal, family or household use as security for repayment of the obligation.

Note: As Official Comment 7 mentions, a "consumer goods transaction" (see 9–102(a)(24)) is included within the definition of a "consumer transaction."

9–102(a)(27)

A "**continuation statement**" is a filing that amends a financing statement by providing the file number of the initial financing statement and indicating that it continues or is filed to continue the effectiveness of the initial financing statement.

9–102(a)(28)

The "**debtor**" is the person who has an interest in the collateral. This person may or may not be the obligor on the obligation to which the security interest in favor of the secured party applies. This is an important distinction, because many people assume that a "debtor" is someone who owes money to the creditor. In Article Nine parlance, this is not correct! The "debtor" *may* be a person who incurs an obligation, but this is not required. All that is required to be an Article Nine debtor is to have an interest in collateral that you put up to cover your own or someone else's obligation.

Note: A debtor's interest in collateral is *not* a security interest or a lien.

Example: A loans $5,000 to B. B's sister S agrees that her diamond necklace will serve as collateral for this loan. S is the debtor—she owns the collateral ("has an interest" in it), but B is the obligor (see 9–102(a)(59)) because B owes the money to A. A is the secured party—his interest in the necklace (collateral) *is* a security interest.

Example: A loans $5,000 to B, who agrees that her diamond necklace will serve as collateral for this loan. B is both the debtor (because she owns/has an interest in the diamond necklace) and the obligor (because she owes the money to A). A is still the secured party.

The term "debtor" also identifies someone who sells accounts, chattel paper, payment intangibles or promissory notes, and further identifies the consignee in a 9–102(a)(20) consignment.

Note: When Article 9 designates someone as a "debtor," it's saying they would not have to take any perfection actions. Instead, their counterpart, the secured party, buyer or consignor, is the one to take perfection steps if they choose to do so.

Example: The seller of accounts is the "debtor" and doesn't have to be concerned about taking perfection steps; the buyer of accounts is designated as a "secured party," and if the buyer wants to protect itself to the greatest degree possible, it's the buyer who should take perfection steps.

9–102(a)(29)

A "**deposit account**" is a savings, checking or other similar account a customer has at a bank. A deposit account is *not* "investment property" or accounts that are evidenced by an instrument, such as a promissory note.

9–102(a)(30)

A "**document**" is a document of title (*not* a certificate of title) or a receipt under 7–201(b), which basically means the holder of the document has the exclusive right to get access to the goods covered by the document.

Example: Warehouse receipts and bills of lading are examples of what Article Nine calls "documents."

9–102(a)(31)

"**Electronic chattel paper**" is a computer-stored record of chattel paper.

Note: See 9–102(a)(11) for the definition of "chattel paper."

9–102(a)(32)

An "**encumbrancer**" is someone with a non-ownership interest—such as a mortgage or other lien—in real estate.

Note: An "encumbrance" serves the same functions as a security interest, but encumbrances are not covered by Article Nine because real estate serves as the collateral, and real estate collateral is excluded from Article Nine coverage.

9–102(a)(33)

"**Equipment**" is a category of collateral that consists of any goods that don't fit under the categories of inventory, farm products or consumer goods.

Example: An office copy machine is equipment because it doesn't fit under any of the other categories. It's not inventory (see 9–102(a)(48)), because it has a relatively long useful life (we hope). It's not farm products (see 9–102(a)(34)), because it's being used in an office rather than a farming operation. It's not consumer goods (see 9–102(a)(23)) because it's being used in an office rather than for personal use.

9–102(a)(34)

"**Farm products**" are goods (other than standing timber) where the debtor is a farmer and where the goods are:

(A) crops that have grown or are growing or will be grown. This includes crops on trees, vines and bushes and aquatic crops produced on aquacultural farms;

(B) livestock, whether or not they've been born. This includes fish or other aquacultural-raised water creatures;

(C) supplies used up or produced in a farming operation; or

(D) products of crops or livestock before the products have undergone a manufacturing process.

Note: A farmer's tractor, which has longer-term use, is equipment. It is *not* considered to be "supplies" (and thus not "farm products") because it has a long useful life and is not quickly used up in the farming operation.

9–102(a)(35)

"**Farming operation**" means any kind of farming, ranching or aquacultural operation.

9–102(a)(36)

The "**file number**" is the number the filing office assigns to an initial financing statement under 9–519(a).

9–102(a)(37)

The "**filing office**" is the office the state designates in 9–501 as the place to file a financing statement.

9–102(a)(38)

A "**filing office rule**" is a rule the filing office adopts to govern its operations as permitted under 9–526.

9–102(a)(39)

The "**financing statement**" is a record or records that consist of the initial financing statement and anything related to it that gets filed with a filing office.

Note: You can find an example of what a financing statement looks like in 9–521.

9–102(a)(40)

A "**fixture filing**" is a filed financing statement for goods that are, or are going to be, fixtures, so long as the filing satisfies 9–502(a) and (b). A "fixture filing" includes a financing statement that covers goods of a "transmitting utility" (such as a railroad or a power company) that are going to become fixtures.

Note: A mortgage may serve as a fixture filing as long as it satisfies 9–502(a) and (b).

9–102(a)(41)

"**Fixtures**" are goods that relate to real estate in such a way that state law says they fall under real estate law.

Note: This is a very general definition. That's because Article Nine leaves it to state property law to more precisely define fixtures. This means that, in practice, you'll need to check the property law of the state where the potential fixture is located to determine if something is, or is not, a fixture under that state's law.

9–102(a)(42)

"**General intangible**" is the catchall category for non-tangible things, including things in action (e.g., the right to sue), payment intangibles and software. You can also say that a general intangible is all personal property *except* for: accounts, chattel paper, commercial tort claims, deposit accounts, documents, goods (tangible things), instruments, investment property, letter-of-credit rights, letters of credit, money and oil, gas or other minerals before they're extracted.

9–102(a)(43)

This space is reserved for a future definition we can fit in here. It used to be the definition of "good faith," but we stuck that somewhere else.

9–102(a)(44)

"**Goods**" means things that, as of the time a security interest attaches to them, are movable physical objects that aren't in some other category (such as things like a promissory note, which may have a physical embodiment but relates to an intangible right).

What are the things that may be physical in some way, but aren't goods? Here's the list:

- accounts and general intangibles. We mention these just to make sure there's no confusion, even if they don't have a physical component.
- Chattel paper
- Commercial tort claims
- Deposit accounts
- Documents
- Instruments
- Investment property
- Letter-of-credit rights
- Letters of credit
- Money
- Oil, gas or other minerals before they're extracted

However, among other things, "goods" *does* include:

(i) fixtures,

(ii) trees before they're cut down as part of a transfer of ownership or under a sales contract,

(iii) the unborn babies of animals,

(iv) crops that are growing or will be grown, even if the crops are on trees, vines or bushes (compare this one to "farm products").

The definition of "goods" covers consumer goods, equipment, farm products and inventory. Computer programs and the information that helps run the programs *may* be in the definition of "goods" if they're embedded in the goods and if the program is so integrated into the goods that it's generally considered part of them.

Example: A computer program that is pre-loaded into a computer is "embedded" in the good (computer). If that program is embedded into the computer you use at your business, it is "equipment" (a type of good) because the computer is equipment.

Computer programs are also "goods" if the owner of the goods they relate to has the right to use the program with the goods simply by virtue of getting ownership of the goods.

Example: If buying a computer automatically grants the buyer the right to use un-embedded programs associated with it, then those programs are treated as if they're the computer itself. They are thus "goods."

However, a computer program is not "goods" if it exists only in the medium that holds it.

Example: A computer program that exists only in a CD used to convey the program for downloading, or only on a server from which the program may be accessed for download, is not considered "goods." Instead, a computer program in either of those instances is "software."

9–102(a)(45)

A "**governmental unit**" is any unit of government of the United States, a State, or a foreign country. It also includes organizations that have their own separate corporate existence if the organizations are eligible to issue debt to investors and the investors don't have to pay income tax on the interest the organizations pay to the investors as part of the debt arrangement.

Example: A non-government development company that issues bonds with tax-free interest is considered a "governmental unit" for Article Nine purposes.

9–102(a)(46)

A "**health care insurance receivable**" is a right to get paid by an insurance company for medical services that have been, or are going to be, provided.

Example: A doctor who treats a patient and has the right to be paid by the patient's health insurer has a "health care insurance receivable." The doctor may have this right directly, or she may have an interest in the patient's right to be paid by the insurer for medical expenses. Either way, it's a health care insurance receivable.

9–102(a)(47)

An "**instrument**" is a negotiable instrument or any other written thing that shows a right to the payment of a monetary obligation *if* it's the type of writing that in the ordinary course of business is transferred with a signature or other indorsement on it.

Note: Articles Three and Four of the UCC deal with negotiable instruments in depth.

Note: Any writing that contains a security agreement or is a lease is not an "instrument," even if it otherwise seems to fit the definition. Also, investment property, letters of credit and writings that are part of charge card transactions are not instruments.

Example: Negotiable promissory notes and checks are "instruments" under 9–102(a)(47).

9–102(a)(48)

"**Inventory**" is goods (tangible things) other than farm products, which:

(A) are leased by a person as a lessor;

(B) are held by a person for sale or lease or will be provided to someone under a service contract;

(C) are actually provided under a service contract; or

(D) are raw materials, including things that are being worked on to create a finished product (also known as "work in progress") or materials that a business uses or consumes

Examples: Pencils or stationary are inventory because they are materials that a business uses or consumes. They are not considered equipment because items that constitute equipment have a relatively longer-term use.

9–102(a)(49)

"**Investment property**" is:

- a security, like stock in a company or bonds issued by a company or a government. The security can be printed on paper, or it may exist only digitally.
- a "security entitlement," which is a right to direct what should be done with the security, such as buying or selling it, even if the security is held in an account under someone else's name.
- a securities account (as opposed to the individual security itself).
- a commodities contract or account.

Note: Article Eight deals in more depth with the non-secured transactions rules and mechanics of investment property.

9–102(a)(50)

The "**jurisdiction of organization**" of a "registered organization" is the State, country or other jurisdiction where the organization was organized.

Example: A Delaware corporation is organized and registered in Delaware, so that State (Delaware) is the jurisdiction of the registered organization.

9–102(a)(61)

A "**payment intangible**" is a general intangible where the account debtor's principal obligation is to repay *money* (as opposed to, for example, perform a service or sell goods).

An "account" is not a payment intangible.

A payment intangible may arise from things like a promissory note or chattel paper where the obligation to pay may be separately broken out from the writing itself. In other words, a payment intangible is the right to receive payment due from the account debtor, but not necessarily the right to enforce the underlying agreement in which the account debtor took on the obligation. Some other party may be holding the original agreement with the debtor and will have the right to enforce it against the debtor if the debtor fails to pay.

The secured party in a payment intangible may only enforce the right to have payments passed along to it, and it would enforce that right against the party holding onto the original agreement if that party doesn't pass along the debtor's payments.

9–102(a)(62)

When we say an individual (a human being) is a "**person related to**" someone, we mean they are that someone's:

(A) spouse; or

(B) brother or sister, or brother-in-law or sister-in-law; or

(C) ancestor or lineal descendant either of themselves or their spouse; or

(D) relative, by blood or marriage, through themselves or their spouse, who shares the same home with the individual.

9–102(a)(63)

When we say a "**person [is] related to**" an organization we mean they are:

(A) directly or indirectly controlling or controlled by the organization or else are under common control with the organization; or

(B) the organization's officer, director or similar person; or

(C) an officer or director of a person controlling or controlled by or under common control with the organization, or a person that performs functions like the ones covered in (A); or

(D) the spouse of an individual who fits the descriptions in (A), (B), or (C); or

(E) someone who shares a home with an individual who fits the descriptions in (A)–(D), and who is related by blood or marriage to that individual.

9–102(a)(64)

"**Proceeds**," except when we use the term in 9–609(b), is:

(A) whatever is acquired when the collateral is disposed of in any way (sale, lease, exchange, etc.); or

(B) whatever gets collected on, or distributed because of, the collateral; or

(C) rights that arise from the collateral; or

(D) claims arising from loss or damage to, or defects in, the collateral, or nonconformity or an infringement of use of the collateral, or things similar to this; or

(E) an insurance settlement payable to the debtor or secured party because of loss or damage to, or defect or nonconformity of, the collateral.

Example: If the collateral is an account, payments made by the debtor on the account are proceeds of the collateral under (B).

Example: If the collateral is investment property like securities, dividends paid on the stock are proceeds of the collateral under (B).

9–102(a)(65)

A "**promissory note**" is an instrument that evidences a promise to pay money, but not one that is simply an order to pay or a writing that simply says a bank has received money to be deposited there.

9–102(a)(66)

A "**proposal**" is a record the secured party authenticates that includes the terms on which the secured party is willing to accept collateral in full or partial satisfaction of the secured obligation after the debtor defaults. See 9–620 to 9–626 for more.

9–102(a)(67)

A "**public finance transaction**" means a secured transaction where:

(A) debt securities (bonds, etc.) are issued that

(B) have an initial maturity date of at least 20 years and

(C) the debtor, obligor or anyone else obligated on the collateral is a State or a unit of a State.

9–102(a)(68)

A "**public organic record**" is a record the public can access that is:

(A) the initial record filed with or issued by a State or the U.S. Congress to form or organize an organization, and any record that amends or restates that initial record; or

(B) the initial record of a business trust and any amendment or restatement of that initial record filed with a State under a State statute that requires filings for those kinds of trusts; or

(C) a State or Congressional statute that forms or organizes an organization, along with any filed record that amends the legislation or restates the name of the organization.

9–102(a)(69)

An advance of money or other value is "**pursuant to commitment**" if the secured party makes the advance because it's obligated to do so by agreement, even if a default or other event outside the secured party's control means the secured party, now or in the future, won't have to follow through on its obligation.

9–102(a)(70)

A "**record**" is information placed on something tangible or stored in an electronic or other medium from which it may be retrieved in legible form.

Note: We don't apply this meaning of "record" when we use phrases like "for record," "of record," "record or legal title," and "record owner."

9–102(a)(71)

A "**registered organization**" is one organized solely under the law of a single State or the United States for which the State or the U.S. must maintain the organic record showing that the organization was actually organized. This applies to business trusts formed or organized under the law of a single State if a State statute requires the trust to file its organic record with the State.

Note: A "registered organization" includes corporations, limited liability companies, limited partnerships, and other organizations that by law must register themselves in order to have a legal existence.

Note: A "registered organization" does *not* include partnerships under the Uniform Partnership Act or situations where a business certificate is issued when a trade name is registered. That's because these things don't *require* the relevant government entity to maintain records regarding the partnership or "d/b/a" designation; doing so is *voluntary* on the part of the business.

9–102(a)(72)

A "**secondary obligor**" is a person who:

(A) is secondary to the primary obligor in the sense that the secondary obligor is called on to perform only if the primary obligor doesn't do what it said it would do; or

(B) has the right to go back against a debtor or another obligor or their property if the secondary obligor is called on to perform.

Example: A guarantor is a secondary obligor.

9–102(a)(73)

A "**secured party**" is:

(A) a person in whose favor a security interest is created or provided for in a security agreement, even if an obligation to be secured is not outstanding; or

(B) a person who holds an agricultural lien; or

(C) a consignor, if the consignment arrangement is the type that falls within the checklist of 9–102(a)(20) for Article Nine coverage; or

(D) a person who buys accounts, chattel paper, payment intangibles or promissory notes; or

(E) a trustee, indenture trustee, agent, collateral agent or other representative for whom a security interest or agricultural lien is created or provided for; or

(F) a person who holds a security interest because of special sales, purchase, leasing or banking and instruments rules under 2–401, 2–505, 2–711(3), 2A–508(5), 4–210 or 5–118.

Note: Take a look at the explanation at the end of our 9–102(a)(28) definition of "debtor" for the distinction between secured party and debtor in the context of the *sale* of things like accounts, chattel paper, etc.

9–102(a)(74)

A "**security agreement**" is an agreement that creates or provides for a security interest as defined in 1–201(b)(35).

9–102(a)(75)

When we use the word "**send**" regarding a record or notification, we mean the sender either:

(A) deposited it in the mail, delivered it for transmission or transmitted it by any usual communication method, with proper postage or transmission cost paid, to an appropriate address; or

(B) caused the item to be received within the time it would have been received if it was properly sent under (A).

9–102(a)(76)

"**Software**" is a computer program and its supporting information that facilitates the program's operation.

Note: This definition does not include software when it's a computer program included in the definition of "goods." This means that "software" is free-standing computer programming information that is embedded in a CD-ROM or other medium such as a server, but is not yet loaded into a good like a computer.

9–102(a)(77)

"**State**" means any of the United States, the District of Columbia, Puerto Rico, the U.S. Virgin Islands or any territory or insular possession subject to U.S. jurisdiction.

9–102(a)(78)

A "**supporting obligation**" is a letter of credit right or a secondary obligation (such as a guaranty) that supports payment or performance of an account, instrument, investment property, chattel paper, document or general intangible.

Note: 9–109(b) says that a supporting obligation such as a real estate mortgage that helps assure payment of a promissory note may be brought under the coverage of Article Nine if a security interest is taken in the note.

9–102(a)(79)

"**Tangible chattel paper**" is chattel paper in writing.

9–102(a)(80)

A "**termination statement**" is an amendment to a financing statement that both:

(A) identifies by file number the initial financing statement it's terminating; and

(B) says it's a termination statement or says the initial financing statement is no longer effective.

9–102(a)(81)

A "**transmitting utility**" is a person that primarily operates:

(A) trains, subways and the like;

(B) communications systems that transmit things electronically, electromagnetically or by fiber optics;

(C) pipeline or sewer transmission systems; or

(D) systems that transmit or produce electricity, steam, gas or water.

9–102(b)

This section is a reference to a whole bunch of definitions in other UCC Articles regarding "control" methods of perfection. You don't need us to restate it from the original.

9–102(c)

Article One's general definitions and principles of construction and interpretation apply to Article Nine.

9–103: PURCHASE-MONEY SECURITY INTERESTS

(a) To help us understand what a purchase-money security interest is, we must first define some terms:

(1) the term "purchase-money collateral" means goods or software used as collateral to secure credit extended so the debtor can either purchase or get the right to use the collateral. The "credit extended" could be a money loan or just a seller granting credit (e.g. extra time to pay) to a buyer.

(2) the term "purchase-money obligation" means the value of the debt (i.e., the money loan or grant of credit to a buyer) that the obligor incurred to fund all or part of the transaction that gets it rights in the collateral or allows it to use the collateral, so long as the value given is actually applied to get the rights or use.

(b) A security interest in goods is a purchase-money security interest if:

(1) the goods actually were purchased with the credit extended, using those goods as collateral; or if

(2) & (3) the security interest is in inventory or software that is part of a whole series of purchase-money collateral transactions between the same parties in which all of the goods or software sold over time is supposed to serve as collateral for the other credit arrangements between the parties.

Note: This provision applies to situations such as when a wholesaler extends credit to a retailer for the retailer's purchases that will take place over time. If read literally, 9–103(b)(1) would say that if the first items secured the amounts due for later items, the first items would not be purchase-money security interests because the retailer isn't using only "those goods" as collateral. That result isn't what we intend, so 9–103(b)(2)–(3) are the drafters' attempts to make this clear.

(c) A security interest in software is a purchase-money security interest to the extent it also is used as security for the purchase of goods (separate from the software) in which the secured party has a purchase-money security interest if

(1) the debtor gets the software as part of the transaction in which it gets the goods (e.g., a computer) and

(2) the debtor gets the software mainly because it plans to use the software in the goods.

(d) When someone consigns goods to another person for sale and the consignment falls under Article Nine, that creates a purchase-money security interest in the consigned goods. See 9–102(a)(20) for Article Nine's special definition of "consignment."

(e) Sometimes, part of a security interest is purchase-money, and part is not. Depending on how we apply them, payments that are made are sometimes used to reduce the purchase-money portion of a security interest and sometimes used to reduce the non-purchase-money portion. When payment application is an issue in *non-consumer* situations, we use the following rules:

(1) if the parties agree to a reasonable method of application, then use that method.

(2) if the parties don't agree, use the obligor's intention before or at the time of payment if that can be determined.

(3) if the parties don't agree and you can't tell the obligor's intent, then apply the payments this way:

(A) first to obligations that have no security interest at all;

(B) after that, if there's more than one obligation, then first apply payments to purchase-money security interests in the order in which the security interests were incurred.

(f) When we're dealing with *non-consumer* goods transactions, a purchase-money security interest does not lose its status even if:

(1) the purchase-money collateral is also used to secure a non-purchase-money obligation;

(2) non-purchase-money collateral is also being used to secure the purchase-money obligation; or

(3) the original purchase-money obligation technically ceases to exist because it was renewed, refinanced, consolidated into other obligations or restructured.

(g) In a *non-consumer* goods transaction, whoever claims a purchase-money security interest has the burden of proving the extent of their claimed interest.

(h) It's up to the courts to determine the right rules to apply in consumer goods transactions. The courts shouldn't infer from the rules set out in 9–103(e)–(g) any limitations to apply in consumer goods cases, and they may keep applying already-established rules in those cases.

Examples of a purchase-money security interest:

1. Buyer and Seller agree that Buyer will purchase a car from Seller on credit. Buyer signs an agreement promising to make monthly payments to Seller and to grant Seller a security interest in the car that Buyer is purchasing from Seller to secure Buyer's obligation to make the monthly payments. Seller has taken a purchase-money security interest in the car it sold to Buyer.

2. Buyer and Seller agree that Buyer will purchase a car from Seller. To finance this purchase, Buyer takes out a loan from Bank and grants Bank a security interest in the car Buyer is purchasing to secure Buyer's obligation to make monthly payments on the bank loan. At the time of sale, Bank issues a check to Seller to enable Buyer to purchase the car. Bank has taken a purchase-money security interest in the car.

9–104: WHEN A SECURED PARTY HAS "CONTROL" OVER A DEPOSIT ACCOUNT

(a) A secured party "controls" a deposit account if:

(1) it's the bank where the deposit account is maintained;

(2) the debtor, the secured party and the bank authenticate a record that says the bank will follow the secured party's instructions about what to do with the money in the deposit account without having to get the debtor's consent; or

(3) the secured party becomes the bank's customer on the deposit account along with the original deposit customer.

Example: A bank gets automatic control status over its customer's deposit accounts under 9–104(a)(1) when the customer owes a debt to the bank that is secured by the bank account.

(b) A secured party who establishes control under 9–104(a) still has "control" even if a debtor retains the right to dispose of money in the deposit account.

9–105: WHEN A SECURED PARTY HAS "CONTROL" OVER ELECTRONIC CHATTEL PAPER

A secured party has "control" of electronic chattel paper if the records that make up the chattel paper are created, stored and signed in such a way that:

(1) a single, authoritative copy exists that is unique, identifiable and unalterable (except as allowed in 9–105(4)–(6));

(2) the authoritative copy identifies the secured party as the assignee of the record;

(3) the authoritative copy is sent to and maintained by the secured party or its designated custodian;

(4) the secured party must participate in copies or revisions that add or change an identified assignee of the authoritative copy;

(5) each copy of the authoritative copy—and even a copy of a copy—is readily identifiable as not authoritative; and

(6) any revision of the authoritative copy is readily identifiable as being an authorized or unauthorized revision.

Here is a checklist to see if a secured party has control of electronic chattel paper:

1. Is there only one authoritative copy that is unique, identifiable and unalterable (except as you're told is okay in 9–105(4)–(6))?
2. Does the authoritative copy identify the secured party as the assignee of the copy?
3. Does the secured party or its designated custodian maintain the record?
4. Does the secured party have to be part of any copies or revisions that add or change who is the identified assignee of the authoritative copy?
5. If copies of the authoritative record are to be made, is the system set up so that any copy of that record will clearly be shown to be a copy?
6. If a revision to the authoritative record is to be made, does the revision process clearly show that the revision is authorized (or not authorized, if that's the case)?

If the answer is "yes" to each question on this checklist, then the secured party has control of the electronic chattel paper.

9–106: WHEN A PERSON HAS "CONTROL" OVER INVESTMENT PROPERTY

(a) Look at 8–106 to see how a person gets "control" of a certificated or uncertificated security or a security entitlement.

(b) A secured party controls a commodity contract if:

(1) the secured party is the commodity intermediary that carries the contract. In this case, control is automatic; or

(2) the commodity customer (the debtor), the secured party and the commodity intermediary agree that the intermediary will apply any value distributed from the contract in whatever way the secured party directs without needing the commodity customer's further consent.

(c) A secured party that has control of all security entitlements or commodity contracts carried in a securities or commodities account also has control over the account itself.

9–107: WHEN A SECURED PARTY HAS "CONTROL" OVER A LETTER OF CREDIT RIGHT

A secured party has "control" of a letter of credit right to the extent of any right to payment or performance under the letter if the letter's "issuer" or "nominated person" *consents* to the assignment of proceeds via the rule in 5–114(c) or other applicable law. Check Article Five for the definitions of "issuer" and "nominated person."

9–108: HOW TO DESCRIBE COLLATERAL

Other than the rules in (c), (d) and (e), a description of personal or real property is sufficient, even if it's not specific, as long as it reasonably identifies what it describes.

Note: 9–504(2) allows for the description in the *financing statement* to be broader than what is implied here, so if you are dealing with a financing statement (as opposed to, say, a security agreement), make sure to look at that section as well.

(b) Other than the provisions of (d), a description of collateral reasonably identifies the collateral if the description is:

(1) one that specifically lists the items of collateral; or

(2) a category of collateral; or

(3) except as noted in (c), a type of collateral defined in the UCC; or

(4) of a quantity of whatever descriptive terms are used; or

(5) a computational or allocative formula or procedure to figure out what's covered; or

(6) except as provided in (c), any other method that allows you to objectively determine what property is serving as collateral.

(c) A supergeneric description such as "all the debtor's assets" or "all the debtor's personal property" does *not* reasonably identify the collateral, unless the description is in a financing statement, per 9–504(2).

(d) Other than the rules in (e), a description of a security entitlement or a securities or commodity account is sufficient if it describes:

(1) the collateral using those terms or by saying "investment property," or

(2) the underlying financial asset (specific stocks, bonds, etc.) or commodity contract.

(e) A description only by the type of collateral defined in the UCC is *not* sufficient if it's describing:

(1) a commercial tort claim; or

(2) consumer goods, or a security entitlement or a securities or commodity account in the context of a consumer transaction.

Note: A description of a commercial tort claim needs at least a description of the event that gave rise to the claim. Just saying something like "all commercial tort claims now existing or arising in the future" isn't good enough.

Note: You need a specific listing of the property if you're dealing in the consumer context. So, for example, you shouldn't describe the collateral as "all consumer goods," but you could describe consumer collateral as "all of the debtor's rings, watches, necklaces, and bracelets."

9–109: THE SCOPE OF ARTICLE NINE

(a) Except for the rules in (c) and (d), here is what Article Nine applies to:

(1) a transaction, no matter what form it takes, that creates a "security interest" in personal property or fixtures by contract. "By contract" just means that the creation of a security interest is consensual, as opposed to an interest that automatically arises under non-UCC law;

(2) an agricultural lien;

(3) a *sale* of accounts, chattel paper, payment intangibles or promissory notes;

(4) a consignment with the characteristics listed in 9–102(a)(20);

(5) a security interest that comes about automatically because of special situations involving sales and leasing (2–401, 2–505, 2–711(3), or 2A–508(5)) subject to the rules of 9–110; and

(6) a security interest in certain transactions involving banking (4–210) and letters of credit (5–118).

(b) If an obligation is secured by a type of transaction or interest that is not covered by Article Nine, that doesn't stop Article Nine from applying to an Article Nine transaction where the obligation itself is the security interest.

Example: Say a debtor who has a right to be paid under a promissory note uses that note as security for a loan. If there is a mortgage that accompanies the promissory note, Article Nine applies, allowing the secured party to have the right in the mortgage follow its right in the promissory note as collateral. This is so even though the mortgage is part of a real estate interest, and real estate collateral is not covered by Article Nine. Look at 9–203(g) and 9–308(d) to see how Article Nine drags the supporting real estate interest into its scope when the secured party's security interest is in the promissory note. Look at Official Comment 7 to 9–109 to see how this operates so that a secured party in this situation would not have to make a real estate filing in order to preserve its interests in both the promissory note and the mortgage.

(c) Article Nine doesn't apply if:

(1) it's preempted by a U.S. statute, regulation or treaty;

(2) another statute of this State says its rules control security interests created by this State or a governmental unit of this State;

(3) a statute of another State, foreign country or governmental unit of either says its rules control security interests created by the State, country or governmental unit as part of its own transactions, so long as the statute isn't just dealing with all types of security interests, even those beyond the ones created by the State, country or unit; or

(4) letter of credit law under 5–114 says certain parties have separate and superior rights to the ones in Article Nine.

(d) Article Nine doesn't apply to:

(1) a landlord's lien, unless it's an agricultural lien;

(2) a lien (other than an agricultural lien) that governs services or materials under another statute or rule of law, although 9–333 applies to establish the priority of that lien when it's competing with an Article Nine security interest;

(3) an assignment of a claim for wages, salary or other compensation of an employee (as opposed to an independent contractor);

(4) a *sale* of accounts, chattel paper, payment intangibles or promissory notes if the sale is part of the sale of the business from which they arose;

(5) an assignment of accounts, chattel paper, payment intangibles or promissory notes if they're assigned just for purposes of collection;

(6) an assignment of a right to be paid on a contract if the person who the right is assigned to also is obligated to perform the contract, and is not just getting the right to collect the money owed under the contract;

(7) an assignment of a *single* account, payment intangible or promissory note if the assignment is made to pay off all or part of a *pre-existing* debt;

(8) a transfer of an interest in or assignment of a claim under an insurance policy, unless the policy involves either:

a health care provider that's getting or making an assignment of a health-care-insurance-receivable, i.e., a right to get paid under a patient's insurance policy or any later right to payment for services it provided; or

payments as proceeds from an insurance policy covering damage or destruction of collateral as covered under 9–315 and 9–322;

(9) an assignment of rights under a court judgment, unless it's a judgment that involves a right to payment (such as an account) that was being used as collateral;

(10) a right to recoupment or set-off, but:

(A) use 9–340 when it comes to its effectiveness against deposit accounts, and

(B) use 9–404 when it comes to an account debtor's defenses or claims;

(11) creating or transferring an interest in or lien on real estate, including a lease or the rents due on a lease, except to the extent that these things are covered by:

(A) liens on real estate in 9–203 and 9–308;

(B) fixtures in 9–334;

(C) fixture filings in 9–501, 9–502, 9–512, and 9–516; and

(D) security agreements that cover personal and real property in default and repossession situations in 9–604;

(12) assigning a tort claim, but 9–315 and 9–322 will cover proceeds and priority in proceeds from tort claims;

(13) an assignment of a deposit account as part of a consumer transaction, although proceeds and priorities in proceeds in a consumer deposit account will be covered by 9–315 and 9–322.

Example: 9–109(d)(5) says that Article Nine doesn't apply to a creditor assigning rights to a collection agency to make the agency's job easier by allowing it to pursue collection on its own.

Note: 9–109(d)(9)'s exclusion doesn't apply to lawsuit settlements because those are agreements between the parties, not court judgments. This means that Article Nine *does* cover the use of settlement rights as collateral.

Note: Assignment of a commercial tort claim *is* covered under Article Nine.

Note: Article Nine will apply if a consumer deposit account is used as collateral in a *business* transaction.

9–110: SECURITY INTERESTS INVOLVING ARTICLES 2 AND 2A

Security interests involving special sale and lease situations of goods under 2–401, 2–505, 2–711(3) or 2–508(5) are covered by Article Nine. However, in those situations, until the debtor gets possession of the goods:

(1) the security interest is enforceable even if the attachment requirements of 9–203(b)(3) haven't been met;

(2) filing isn't required to perfect the security interest;

(3) the rights of the secured party after default of the debtor are covered by Articles 2 and 2A; and

(4) the security interest has priority over a conflicting security interest that the debtor created.

INTRODUCTION TO THE 9–200s

The 9–200s (or "Part 2" of Article Nine) discuss attachment and, specifically, the security agreement. Important provisions include the requirements for attachment (i.e., creation) of a security interest (9–203), how after-acquired property is dealt with (9–204), and information on what a secured party in possession of collateral must do with respect to that collateral (9–207). If you have questions about how to create a security interest, the 9–200s should be your first stop.

9–201: THE SECURITY AGREEMENT'S EFFECTIVENESS

(a) Except for where the UCC says otherwise, a security agreement's terms are effective between the secured party and the debtor, and also against other creditors and purchasers of the collateral to the extent our rules say they are effective against these others.

(b) Consumer, usury and similar laws and regulations apply to anything in Article Nine.

(c) Consumer, usury and similar laws and regulations supersede Article Nine's rules if they are in conflict with them.

(d) Article Nine:

(1) does not provide an avenue for anyone to get around rules and restrictions in consumer, usury and similar laws, and

(2) does not provide an avenue to extend those rules or restrictions beyond what they cover.

9–202: "TITLE" DOESN'T MATTER

It doesn't matter whether a debtor or secured party technically has "title" (that is, ownership) to collateral or any other property covered in Article Nine. Instead, Article Nine just cares about whether the party has rights *of some kind* in the collateral, even if those rights aren't the same as having title. Article Nine's rules will control who has the greater priority between an owner and a secured party. Remember, though, there may be special rules for property that is the subject of a consignment, or for sales of accounts, chattel paper, payment intangibles or promissory notes.

Example: A seller sold a piece of equipment on credit, but has retained title until the buyer pays in full. The buyer may have rights in the equipment that are concrete enough to allow it to use the equipment as collateral for its loans, even though the buyer doesn't yet have title or ownership because it hasn't fully paid the seller. So someone who loaned money to the equipment buyer (the debtor) may have the right to get the equipment if (1) their debtor defaults on the loan, (2) the seller of equipment didn't take steps that Article Nine specifies to protect its interest, and (3) there isn't another part of the UCC or other law that protects the seller's interests. This would leave the seller saying, "Hey, that's equipment to which I have title! I own it!" The foreclosing creditor would reply, "Maybe so, but you don't have priority to it any more because the rules favor me over you under these circumstances. Better luck next time."

9–203: REQUIREMENTS FOR ATTACHMENT

(a) A security interest attaches to collateral when what it says about the collateral may be enforced against the debtor. 9–203(b) describes when a security interest may be enforced. The parties may postpone the time of attachment, but they can't accelerate it.

(b) Except as provided in (c)–(i), a security interest's terms involving the collateral are enforceable against the debtor and third parties only if:

(1) value has been given. In other words, the secured party must have given something of "value," defined in 1–204, to justify the debtor's granting of the security interest;

(2) the debtor has rights in the collateral. Remember, per 9–202, this doesn't mean the debtor necessarily has *title* to the collateral, but just that it has some right to grant the security interest; and

(3) at least one of the following conditions is met:

(A) the debtor authenticates a security agreement that describes the collateral (and also the land that timber-to-be-cut is on, if that's the collateral); or

(B) the collateral is in the secured party's possession under the rules of 9–313 governing possession, so long as (1) possession is in accordance with the debtor's agreement and (2) the collateral is not a certificated security; or

Note: This 9–203(b)(3)(B) provision means that a secured party may have an attached security interest so long as it has possession of the collateral under the terms of a security agreement with the debtor, but the agreement doesn't have to be in writing if there's possession. This is the only situation where a security interest may attach based on an oral agreement.

(C) the collateral is a certificated security in registered form and it is delivered to the secured party by following the rules of 8–301 under the terms of the debtor's security agreement; or

(D) the collateral is deposit accounts, electronic chattel paper, investment property, letter-of-credit rights, or electronic documents, and the secured party, per the debtor's security agreement, "controls" the collateral under 7–106, or 9–104 through 9–107.

(c) Section (b) is subject to the rules in 4–210 (a collecting bank's security interest), 5–118 (the security interest of certain letter-of-credit parties), 9–110 (a security interest covered by the sales and lease rules of Articles 2 and 2A), and 9–206 (security interests in investment property).

Note: This provision means that if something in another part of the Code more specifically applies to those types of collateral, you should apply that part instead of the 9–203(b) rules.

(d) A person becomes bound as if they were the debtor on a security agreement that someone else entered into if by contract or other laws outside of Article Nine:

(1) the security agreement becomes effective to create a security interest in the person's property; or

(2) the person becomes generally obligated for the other person's obligations, and acquires or succeeds to all or substantially all of the other person's assets

Example: By operation of state corporate merger law, one corporation can become generally obligated for another's obligations and/or acquire or succeed to all or substantially all of the other corporation's assets.

(e) If a "new debtor" (see 9–102(a)(56)) becomes bound by a security agreement entered into by someone else:

(1) the agreement satisfies (b)(3) when it comes to existing or after-acquired property of the new debtor so long as the property is described in the agreement; and

(2) you can use the old agreement without having to make a whole new one.

(f) Once a security agreement attaches to collateral, it automatically gives the secured party the rights to proceeds under 9–315 and also attaches to a supporting obligation for the collateral

Example: A third party's guarantee of payment that applies to a promissory note is a "supporting obligation."

(g) If an obligation that is secured by a security interest or other lien on personal or real estate is transferred, then the security interest or lien is automatically transferred as well.

(h) & (i) If a security interest attaches to a securities or commodity account, then it also automatically attaches to the securities entitlements or commodity contracts that are *in* the account.

9–204: ATTACHMENT OF AFTER-ACQUIRED COLLATERAL

(a) A security agreement may provide that it applies to after-acquired collateral, subject to the limitations in (b), below.

(b) A security interest does not attach under an after-acquired property clause:

(1) if the collateral is consumer goods acquired more than 10 days after the secured party gave value, except for accessions (9–335) when they are given as additional security added to the original collateral, or

(2) to a commercial tort claim

Note: A secured party must specify *which* commercial tort claim(s) is (are) covered rather than just saying the security interest applies to "all future tort claims."

(c) A security interest may provide that the collateral covers future advances of money or giving of other value even if the secured party hasn't committed to make a later advance or to give other value. This applies to sales of accounts, chattel paper, payment intangibles or promissory notes: these things may serve as collateral for future advances of funds to cover future sales, at least insofar as Article Nine applies to sales of those things.

Note: For convenience, Article Nine says the seller of accounts, chattel paper, payment intangibles or promissory notes is a "debtor," and the buyer is a "secured party." The idea is to make the secured party/buyer aware that it may have to take perfection steps (or that it may benefit from automatic or temporary perfection), even though it is not extending credit to the seller/debtor. Article Nine's designation of these titles to the buyer and seller is desirable because, although Article Nine is usually thought to apply to transactions involving credit, in fact it also covers sales of certain kinds of assets such as the ones listed here. If Article Nine didn't make these designations, we would need to create other names for the parties in these situations, but the rules that apply would be repetitive of the usual credit-type security interest situations. Hence the efficiency of simply saying, "Hey buyer, we're calling you a secured party, which means you're the one who has to think about whether you need to take more Article Nine steps if you want to protect yourself to the greatest possible degree."

9–205: THE SECURITY INTEREST IS STILL ATTACHED IN THESE SITUATIONS

(a) A security interest is still valid if the only complaint is that the situation could mislead other creditors because:

(1) the debtor is allowed:

(A) to use or get rid of all or part of the collateral; or

(B) to collect on or negotiate over the collateral; or

(C) accept the return of the collateral or make repossessions; or

(D) to do anything it wants with the proceeds of the collateral; or

Example: If the debtor is allowed to collect on accounts that are serving as collateral and to deal with the account debtors who owe on those accounts, a security interest in those accounts is still valid.

Example: Let's say the collateral is inventory, and the debtor is a retailer who sells the inventory on credit. A security interest is still valid if the debtor is permitted to repossess the inventory in the event its buyer doesn't pay.

(2) the secured party doesn't make the debtor account for proceeds or replace collateral that is disposed of by the debtor.

(b) This section doesn't relax the requirement of possession if attachment, perfection or enforcement of a security interest depends on possession of the collateral by the secured party.

9–206: SECURITY INTERESTS IN CERTAIN FINANCIAL ASSETS

(a) A security interest in favor of a securities intermediary, such as a stockbroker, attaches to a person's security entitlement if the person buys a financial asset through the intermediary and is supposed to pay in full at the time of purchase, and the intermediary credits the asset to the buyer's securities account before payment is made.

(b) The security interest described in (a), above, secures the buyer's obligation to pay for the *financial asset*—but not for other debts between the buyer and the intermediary.

(c) A security interest in favor of a person delivering a certificated security or other financial asset represented by a writing attaches to the security or other financial asset if:

(1) the security or other asset typically is indorsed or assigned as part of its transfer process and is delivered under an agreement between persons who deal in those kinds of securities or financial assets; and

(2) the agreement calls for delivery upon payment.

Note: This means that if someone delivers to a buyer a tangible security or other financial asset such as a money market instrument on behalf of a seller, and the buyer is supposed to pay for what is delivered, the deliverer has a security interest that allows it to repossess what was delivered if the buyer doesn't make payment.

(d) The security interest described in (c), above, secures the obligation to make payment to the seller.

9–207: SECURED PARTY'S TREATMENT OF COLLATERAL IN ITS POSSESSION OR CONTROL

(a) Other than as provided in (d), below, a secured party must use reasonable care to preserve collateral in its possession. If the collateral is chattel paper or an instrument, reasonable care includes taking necessary steps to preserve rights against earlier parties who had interests in the collateral. This includes things like getting proper indorsements for transfer.

(b) Other than as provided in (d), below, when a secured party possesses collateral:

(1) the secured party may charge reasonable expenses for the costs it incurs in preserving the collateral. Those expenses are automatically secured by the collateral until reimbursed;

(2) it's the debtor's risk if there's not enough insurance coverage and something bad happens to the collateral;

(3) the secured party should keep the collateral in a way that allows it to be identified, but if one type of item of collateral is the same as another type they can be mixed together; and

(4) the secured party may use or operate the collateral:

(A) to preserve it or maintain its value; or

(B) in any way an authorized court allows; or

(C) in any way the debtor agrees, as long as that follows consumer law rules in the case of consumer goods.

(c) Other than as provided in (d), below, a secured party that possesses or controls collateral under 7–106, 9–104, 9–105, 9–106 or 9–107:

(1) may use proceeds other than money or funds received from the collateral as additional collateral;

(2) must apply money or funds received from the collateral to reduce the secured obligation unless they have been turned over to the debtor; and

(3) may create a security interest in the collateral.

Example: If there is a stock split, the new shares are treated as if they are the same as the old shares.

(d) If the secured party is a buyer of accounts, chattel paper, payment intangibles or promissory notes, or is a consignor:

(1) (a) does not apply unless an agreement allows the secured party:

(A) to charge back uncollected collateral; or

(B) full or limited recourse against the debtor or a secondary obligor, such as a guarantor, if an account debtor or other obligor on the collateral defaults; and

Example: If an account debtor on an account doesn't pay, the secured party can treat that account as not being part of the collateral.

(2) (b) and (c) don't apply.

9–208: HOW A SECURED PARTY RELINQUISHES CONTROL IN CERTAIN PROPERTY ONCE PAID

(a) This section applies to cases where there is no outstanding secured obligation—for example, because the obligor paid it off—and the secured party is not committed to make an advance or give other kinds of value.

(b) Within 10 days of receiving an authenticated demand by the debtor:

(1) a secured party who controls a deposit account under 9–104(a)(2) must send to the bank an authenticated statement that releases the bank from having to follow the secured party's instructions;

(2) a secured party who controls a deposit account under 9–104(a)(3) must:

(A) pay the debtor the balance on deposit in the account; or

(B) transfer the balance on deposit into a deposit account in the debtor's name;

(3) a secured party (that is not a buyer) who has control of electronic chattel paper under 9–105 must:

(A) communicate the authoritative copy of the electronic chattel paper to the debtor or its designated custodian;

(B) if the debtor's custodian is the same one the secured party used as custodian, communicate an authenticated record that tells the custodian it should follow the debtor's instructions from now on and releases the custodian from having to follow the secured party's instructions; and

(C) take whatever action is needed to allow the debtor or its custodian to revise or make copies of the authoritative copy to add or change an assignee of the authoritative copy without the secured party's consent;

(4) if the secured party controls investment property under 8–106(d)(2) or 9–106(b) it must send to the securities or commodities intermediary that maintains it an authenticated record that releases the intermediary from any further obligation to follow entitlement orders or direction from the secured party;

(5) a secured party that controls a letter-of-credit right under 9–107 must send an authenticated release from any further obligation to pay or deliver proceeds to anyone who has an unfulfilled obligation of that type. In other words, the secured party must let the other party know they're off the hook for payment;

(6) a secured party that controls an electronic document must:

(A) give control of the electronic document to the debtor or the debtor's designated custodian;

(B) if the debtor's custodian is the same one the secured party used as custodian, communicate an authenticated record that tells the custodian it should follow the debtor's instructions from now on and releases the custodian from having to follow the secured party's instructions; and

(C) take whatever action is needed to allow the debtor or its custodian to revise or make copies of the authoritative copy to add or change an assignee of the authoritative copy without the secured party's consent.

9–209: ONCE PAID, A SECURED PARTY SHOULD NOTIFY ACCOUNT DEBTORS NOT TO PAY THEM

(a) Except for what's in (c), this section applies to cases where there is no outstanding secured obligation—for example, because the obligor paid it off—and the secured party is not committed to make an advance or give other kinds of value.

(b) Within 10 days after receiving an authenticated demand from the debtor, the secured party must send an authenticated release to an account debtor that has received notice that their account has been assigned to the secured party. In other words, the secured party should let the account debtor know that the secured party no longer has an interest in the account, so the account debtor should deal with the secured party's former debtor from now on.

(c) This section doesn't apply to the sale of an account debtor's obligations on an account, chattel paper or payment intangible. In other words, this section only applies when the account has been used as collateral in a third-party lending or purchase money security interest situation. It doesn't apply when the secured party bought the account outright.

9–210: HOW A DEBTOR GETS INFORMATION FROM A SECURED PARTY ABOUT CERTAIN COLLATERAL

(a) In this section:

(1) "Request" means a record described in (2), (3) or (4), below.

(2) "Request for accounting" means an authenticated record from a debtor that identifies the transaction or relationship involved and that asks the recipient to provide an account of what the debtor still owes on any secured debt.

(3) "Request regarding a list of collateral" means an authenticated record from a debtor that identifies the transaction or relationship involved, and that asks the recipient to approve or correct a list of what the debtor believes to be the collateral securing the obligation.

(4) "Request regarding a statement of account" means an authenticated record from a debtor that identifies the transaction or relationship involved and that asks the recipient to approve or correct the amount the debtor believes is still owed on the obligation.

(b) Except as set forth in (c), (d), (e) and (f), below, a secured party must reply within 14 days after receipt to a request that is:

(1) a request for an accounting by sending an authenticated accounting to the debtor; and

(2) a request regarding a list of collateral or a request regarding a statement of account by sending an authenticated approval or correction.

(c) A secured party that claims a security interest in all of a particular type of collateral owned by the debtor complies with a request regarding a list of collateral if it sends the debtor an authenticated statement that states the claim within 14 days of receiving the request.

(d) If a person receives a request regarding a list of collateral and now claims no interest in the collateral that used to be subject to its claim, then the person has 14 days to reply to the request by sending the debtor an authenticated record that:

(1) says the person has no interest in the collateral, and

(2) gives the name and mailing address of any assignee of or successor to the person's interest in the collateral, if known.

(e) If a person receives a request for an accounting under (a)(2), above, or regarding a statement of account under (a)(4), above, and now claims no interest in the obligations to which the requests apply, then the person has 14 days to reply to the request by sending the debtor an authenticated record that:

(1) says the person has no interest in the obligations, and

(2) gives the name and mailing address of any assignee of or successor to the person's interest in the obligation, if known.

(f) A debtor is entitled to get one free response to a request covered by 9–210 during any six-month period. The secured party may require a payment of up to $25 for each additional response.

INTRODUCTION TO THE 9–300s

The 9–300s (or "Part 3" of Article Nine) deal with perfection and priority. There are a lot of important provisions in these sections. Here you'll find the rules related to the various methods of perfection (filing, possession, control, temporary, and automatic). You'll also find provisions relating to the priority of security interests vis-a-vis other interests, and information on things like fixtures, accessions, and commingled goods. Finally, you'll learn some things a bank can do with a debtor's deposit account.

9–301: WHAT LAW GOVERNS PERFECTION AND PRIORITY FOR SECURITY INTERESTS

(a) Except for what's in 9–303 through 9–306, the following rules determine the law governing perfection, the effect of perfection or non-perfection, and the priority of a security interest in collateral:

(1) Except where we say otherwise in this section, the law of the jurisdiction in which the debtor is located governs the act of perfection, what the effect is of being perfected or not perfected, and the priority of a security interest in collateral.

Note: 9–301(a)(1) is our general rule. It says to use the rules of the **debtor's** jurisdiction for filing, possessory, temporary, automatic and control perfection and for everything else that Article Nine covers unless we say something different.

(2) While collateral is located in a jurisdiction, the law of that jurisdiction governs the act of perfection, what the effect is of being perfected or not perfected and the priority of a *possessory* security interest in the collateral.

Note: There can be many local variations on how priorities change when a possessory interest is involved, so when a secured party has possession of the collateral by agreement with the debtor, 9–301(a)(2) tells us to apply the rules of the collateral's locale to anything covered by Article Nine.

(3) Except for what's in (4), while tangible (not electronic) negotiable documents, goods, instruments, money or tangible (not electronic) chattel paper are in a jurisdiction, the local law of that jurisdiction governs:

(A) perfection of a security interest in goods by a fixture filing;

(B) perfection of a security interest in timber to be cut; and

(C) what it means to be perfected or not perfected and the priority of a *nonpossessory* security interest in the collateral.

Note: *Perfection* is still controlled by the laws of the debtor's jurisdiction per 9–301(a)(1); it is just the *effect* of perfection and *priority* that are governed by the laws of the location of the types of collateral laid out in 9–102(a)(3). This distinguishes the treatment of nonpossessory security interests from 9–301(a)(2)'s rule about possessory interests. This also means that you should use 9–301(a)(1) for all the rules regarding *intangible* collateral. Why? Intangible collateral isn't mentioned in 9–301(a)(2) or (3), so because we haven't been told otherwise, the rules of 9–301(a)(1) must apply to intangible collateral.

(4) The local law where a well head or mine head is located governs perfection, the effect of perfection or non-perfection and the priority of a security interest in as-extracted collateral.

Putting it all together: 9–301

Subsections (a)(1) and (a)(2), alongside (a)(3), taken together mean that when you have a non-possessory security interest, you should file or otherwise perfect using the laws of the debtor's location, but the laws of the location of the collateral apply to the collateral. This is so because, assuming everyone's operating under the same uniform law, applying the laws of the collateral's location will tell you to look at the debtor's location for perfection rules, and the debtor's location's laws will tell you to look via 9–301(a)(3) at the laws of the collateral's location for the other rules. To complete the circle, the laws of the debtor's location will tell you to apply the laws of the location of the collateral when a possessory security interest is involved.

9–302: WHAT LAW GOVERNS PERFECTION AND PRIORITY FOR AGRICULTURAL LIENS

The local law of the jurisdiction where farm products are located governs the effect of perfection or non-perfection and the priority of an agricultural lien on the farm products.

9–303: WHAT LAW GOVERNS PERFECTION AND PRIORITY FOR GOODS COVERED BY A CERTIFICATE OF TITLE

(a) This section applies to goods covered by a certificate of title, even if the jurisdiction that issued the certificate of title has no relationship, other than these rules, to the goods or the debtor.

(b) Goods are covered by a certificate of title when a valid application and fee are delivered to the authority that does the certificating. Goods stop being covered by a certificate of title when the law of the certificating jurisdiction says so, or when the goods later become covered by a certificate of title from another jurisdiction, whichever is earlier.

(c) The law of the jurisdiction whose certificate of title covers the goods controls perfection, the effect of perfection or non-perfection, and the priority of a security interest in the goods during the time the goods are covered.

Note: 9–303(b) and (c), taken together, mean that goods are covered by a certificate of title until another jurisdiction issues a new certificate. At that point, the new certificate is the only one that "covers" the goods. We know this because 9–303(b) says goods stop being "covered" by one certificate once another is issued elsewhere, and 9–303(c) says that once that happens, you just apply the law of the new place that covers the goods.

9–304: WHAT LAW GOVERNS PERFECTION AND PRIORITY FOR DEPOSIT ACCOUNTS

Use the local law of the jurisdiction where a bank is located to govern the act of perfection, what it means to be perfected or not perfected, and the priority of a security interest in a deposit account at that bank.

9–305: WHAT LAW GOVERNS PERFECTION AND PRIORITY FOR INVESTMENT PROPERTY

(a) Except for what we say in (c), below, these rules apply:

(1) The law of the location of a certificated security governs the act of perfection, what it means to be perfected or not perfected, and the priority of a security interest in the certificated security.

(2) Where an uncertificated security is involved, first look at 8–110(d) to identify the jurisdiction of the issuer. The issuer's jurisdiction is the jurisdiction that governs the act of perfection, what it means to be perfected or not perfected, and the priority of a security interest in the uncertificated security.

(3) Where a security entitlement or securities account is involved, first look at 8–110(e) to identify the jurisdiction of the security intermediary. The security intermediary's jurisdiction is the jurisdiction that governs the act of perfection, what it means to be perfected or not perfected, and the priority of a security interest in the security entitlement or securities account.

(4) Where a commodity contract or account is involved, the law of the location of the commodity intermediary governs the act of perfection, what it means to be perfected or not perfected, and the priority of a security interest in the commodity contract or account.

(b) These rules determine a commodity intermediary's jurisdiction for Article Nine purposes:

(1) The parties may expressly agree that a certain jurisdiction is the commodity intermediary's jurisdiction in connection with a commodities account for purposes of Article Nine.

(2) If (b)(1) doesn't apply, the commodity intermediary's jurisdiction is whatever jurisdiction an express agreement between the parties says is the jurisdiction's rules to apply to a commodity account.

(3) If (b)(1) and (b)(2) don't apply, the commodity intermediary's jurisdiction is wherever the parties expressly agree is the location where a commodity account is maintained.

(4) If (b)(1)–(b)(3) don't apply, the commodity intermediary's jurisdiction is whatever location an account statement says is the office serving the customer's account.

(5) If (b)(1)–(b)(4) don't apply, the jurisdiction of the chief executive office of the commodity intermediary is the intermediary's jurisdiction.

(c) The laws of the debtor's jurisdiction governs:

(1) perfection by filing of a security interest in investment property;

(2) automatic perfection of a security interest in investment property that a broker or securities intermediary creates; and

(3) automatic perfection of a security interest in a commodity contract that a commodity intermediary creates.

9–306: WHAT LAW GOVERNS PERFECTION AND PRIORITY FOR LETTER-OF-CREDIT RIGHTS

(a) Except for what we say in (c), below, the local law of the issuer's or a nominated person's jurisdiction governs the act of perfection, what it means to be perfected or not perfected, and the priority of a security interest in a letter-of-credit right, so long as that jurisdiction is a State.

Note: If the jurisdiction is *not* a State, use 9–301 to make the debtor's (beneficiary's) location the jurisdiction whose Article Nine rules govern. This means that one U.S. State jurisdiction's Article Nine rules may apply to a beneficiary's right against a nominated person that is located in that State, but that the debtor/beneficiary's rights against the issuer may be governed by the *debtor's* jurisdiction in the U.S. if, for example, the issuer is located outside the U.S. and the letter of credit says non-U.S. law applies to the issuer's liability.

(b) For our purposes, an issuer's or nominated person's jurisdiction is the jurisdiction under 5–116 whose law governs liability of the issuer or nominated person when it comes to the letter-of-credit right.

(c) This section doesn't apply to a security interest that is perfected only under 9–308(d) as a supporting obligation.

9–307: HOW TO DETERMINE THE DEBTOR'S LOCATION

(a) When we say "place of business" we mean a place where the debtor conducts its affairs.

(b) Except where we say otherwise, here is where a debtor is located:

(1) At their principal residence if the debtor is an individual.

(2) At its place of business if it's an organization (but not a "registered organization") with only one place of business.

(3) At its chief executive office if it's an organization (but not a "registered organization") with more than one place of business.

(c) The rules in (b) only apply if the place where these types of debtors are located is a jurisdiction that generally requires a public notice filing, recording or registration for non-possessory security interests if the interests are to have priority over lien holders. If (b) *doesn't* apply, then the debtor is located in the District of Columbia.

Note: By "generally requires," we mean that the jurisdiction in question generally requires notice in a filing or recording system. However, the jurisdiction can also permit perfection by other methods, such as control, automatic, or temporary perfection, in some circumstances.

(d) A person is still located in the jurisdiction specified in (b) and (c) even if they no longer exist or otherwise don't fit the requirements for existence under those subsections.

(e) A registered organization is located in whichever State it's organized. Put differently, a registered organization is located in whatever State it has filed its single official registration document.

(f) If a registered organization is organized under federal law or in a branch or agency that is not organized under federal or State law, its location is:

(1) in the State that federal law designates, if it designates a State;

(2) in the State the registered organization designates, if federal law allows it to make its own designation;

(3) in the District of Columbia if (f)(1) and (2) don't apply.

(g) Even if a registered organization has its registration suspended, revoked or forfeited, or if it is dissolved, wound up or canceled from existence, its location is still the jurisdiction specified in (e) & (f).

(h) The United States is located in the District of Columbia, for purposes of naming it as a party.

(i) A branch or agency of a non-federal or non-State bank is located in whatever State licenses it, if all branches and agencies of the bank are licensed in only one State.

(j) A foreign air carrier is located at the office of its designated agent for service of process.

(k) This section only determines the debtor's location for choice-of-law purposes.

9–308: WHEN A SECURITY INTEREST OR AGRICULTURAL LIEN IS PERFECTED

(a) Except where we say otherwise here and in 9–309, a security interest is perfected if it has attached and all the perfection requirements in 9–310 through 9–316 have been satisfied. A security interest is perfected when it attaches if all the perfection steps have been taken before the security interest attaches.

(b) An agricultural lien is perfected if it is effective and meets 9–310's applicable perfection requirements. An agricultural lien is perfected when it becomes effective if the perfection steps have been taken before it becomes effective.

(c) A security interest or agricultural lien is continuously perfected even if the method of perfection changes, so long as there's no break in some kind of perfection at any point.

Example: A security interest originally perfected by possession is continuously perfected by a later appropriate filing, even after possession is given up, as long as there's no gap between possession ending and filing starting.

(d) If you perfect a security interest in collateral, you're automatically perfecting a security interest in any supporting obligation, even if the supporting obligation is something that's not otherwise covered by Article Nine.

Example: Imagine that the collateral is a promissory note. If there is a guarantor who promises to pay what's owed on the note if the obligor doesn't pay, a secured party with a perfected security interest in the note *automatically* gets a perfected security interest in the guarantee. This is true even though surety interests like guarantees are not themselves a type of Article Nine collateral.

Note: 9–208(g) provides the parallel rule: getting an *attached* security interest in a type of collateral that Article Nine covers also automatically grants an attached security interest in its supporting obligations.

(e) If you perfect a security interest in a right to payment or performance, you're also perfecting a security interest in a security interest, mortgage or other similar thing on personal or real property that secures the right.

(f) If you perfect a security interest in a securities account, you're also perfecting a security interest in the security entitlements in the account.

(g) If you perfect a security interest in a commodities account, you're also perfecting a security interest in the entitlements in the account.

9–309: AUTOMATIC PERFECTION

These security interests are automatically perfected at the moment they attach. This means that, with respect to these security interests, a secured party doesn't have to take *any* perfection steps:

(1) a purchase money security interest in consumer goods (other than the exceptions in 9–311(b) that may be subject to a law specified in 9–311(a)).

(2) an assignment of accounts or payment intangibles when it's not assigning a significant part of those collateral types. This includes other transfers when combined with those types of things assigned to the same party;

(3) a *sale* of a payment intangible;

(4) a *sale* of a promissory note;

(5) a security interest from an assignment of a health-care-insurance receivable to the health care goods or services provider;

(6) a security interest that automatically attaches under special sales or leasing rules in 2–401, 2–505, 2–711(3) or 2A–508(5), at least until the debtor gets possession of the collateral;

(7) a security of a collecting bank under 4–210;

(8) a security interest of an issuer or nominated person under 5–118 (letters of credit);

(9) a security interest that automatically arises from delivery of a 9–206(c) financial asset;

(10) a security interest that a broker or securities intermediary takes in a client's investment property;

(11) a security interest that a commodity intermediary takes in a client's commodity contract or commodity account;

(12) an assignment of property for the benefit of creditors and later transfers of the same things by the assignee;

(13) a security interest automatically created when a beneficial interest in a decedent's estate is assigned; and

(14) a *sale* by a lottery winner of their right to payment of their winnings.

9–310: WHEN A SECURED PARTY MUST FILE A FINANCING STATEMENT TO PERFECT

(a) A secured party has to file a financing statement to perfect its security interests and agricultural liens, except for the situations in (b), below, and in 9–312(b).

(b) A secured party doesn't have to file a financing statement to perfect its security interest:

(1) if it's perfected automatically under 9–308(d), (e), (f) or (g) because it's a special category of security interest;

(2) that 9–309 says is automatically perfected when it attaches;

(3) that's subject to a 9–311(a) law;

(4) when the collateral is goods in the possession of a bailee and is perfected under 9–312(d)(1) or (2);

(5) when the collateral is certificated securities, documents, goods or instruments that may be perfected without filing, possession or control under 9–312(e), (f) or (g);

(6) in collateral in the secured party's possession under 9–313;

(7) in a certificated security that's perfected by delivering it to the secured party under 9–313;

(8) in deposit accounts, electronic chattel paper, electronic documents, investment property or letter-of-credit rights perfected by control under 9–314;

(9) in proceeds perfected under 9–315; or

(10) that's perfected under 9–316.

9–311: WHEN SPECIAL LAWS APPLY TO PERFECTION

(a) Except for (d), below, a filing is neither necessary nor effective to perfect a security interest subject to:

(1) a U.S. statute, regulation or treaty that preempts 9–310(a) when it comes to obtaining rights over a lien creditor;

(2) [each State's special statutes that govern certificates of title and non-UCC central filings. . .each legislature inserts those here]; or

(3) a certificate-of-title statute from another jurisdiction that requires a security interest to be shown on the certificate of title if it is to get priority over a lien creditor.

(b) Complying with a law described in (a), above, is treated as if it is a filing of a financing statement under Article Nine. Except for (d), below, and 9–313 and 9–316(d) & (e), for certificate-of-title goods a secured party has to follow the rules in laws described in (a), above, if it wants its security interest to be treated as perfected; and if it does so, it will be treated as if it's still perfected even if the use of the property changes, or if possession of the property is transferred.

(c) Except for (d), below, and 9–316(d) & (e), the special laws described in (a), above, control how long the security interest is perfected and when and how it should be renewed. But otherwise, Article Nine applies to the extent the (a) laws don't.

(d) This section doesn't apply to a statute named in (a)(2), above, that covers inventory held for lease or sale by someone who is in the business of leasing or selling that kind of goods.

9–312: PERFECTION (INCLUDING TEMPORARY PERFECTION) OF SECURITY INTERESTS IN CHATTEL PAPER, NEGOTIABLE DOCUMENTS, INSTRUMENTS, INVESTMENT PROPERTY, DEPOSIT ACCOUNTS, LETTER-OF-CREDIT RIGHTS, AND MONEY

(a) You may file to perfect a security interest in chattel paper, negotiable documents, instruments or investment property.

(b) Except for 9–315(c) and (d) regarding proceeds:

(1) you must perfect a security interest in a deposit account only through control under 9–314;

(2) you must perfect a security interest in letter-of-credit rights by control under 9–314, unless you're using 9–308(d);

(3) you must perfect your security interest in money by taking possession under 9–313.

(c) While a bailee that issues a negotiable document has possession of goods that the document covers:

(1) perfecting your security interest in the document also perfects your security interest in the goods;

(2) the security interest perfected in the document has priority over any security interest that becomes perfected in the goods while your perfection in the document is in force.

(d) While a bailee who issues a *non*-negotiable document has possession of goods that the document covers, your security interest in the goods may be perfected by:

(1) having a document issued in your name;

(2) making sure the bailee receives notification of your interest; or

(3) filing to perfect as to the goods.

(e) Your security interest in certificated securities, negotiable documents or instruments is perfected for 20 days from the time it attaches even if you don't file or take possession, if it arises for new value given under an authenticated security agreement.

Note: This is ***not*** an avenue to skirt around the limits on attachment of oral security agreements under 9–203(b).

(f) If you have a perfected security interest in a negotiable document or goods that are in the possession of a bailee other than one who issued a negotiable document for the goods, then your security interest stays perfected for 20 days without filing if you let the debtor get the goods or the document representing the goods, so the debtor may:

(1) ultimately sell or exchange the goods; or

(2) load, store, process, ship or anything else like that in order to get the goods ready to be sold or exchanged.

(g) If you have a perfected security interest in a certificated security or an instrument, then your interest stays perfected for 20 days without filing if you let the debtor get the security or instrument so the debtor may:

(1) sell or exchange them; or

(2) present, collect, enforce, renew or register their transfer.

(h) Once the 20 days specified in (e), (f) or (g) expires, perfection depends on complying with other Article Nine provisions. So, if you want to be continuously perfected past the temporary 20-day perfection period, make sure you're perfected in some other way before the 20 days passes because you cannot extend this temporary perfection.

9–313: PERFECTION BY POSSESSION OR DELIVERY

(a) Except for (b), you can perfect your security interest in tangible negotiable documents, goods, instruments, money, or tangible chattel paper by taking possession of the collateral. You can perfect your security interest in certificated securities by taking delivery of them under 8–301.

(b) When you're dealing with a certificate of title issued by this State, you may perfect your security interest by possession of the goods only in the situations described in 9–316(d).

(c) For collateral other than certificated securities and goods covered by a document, here are the situations when a secured party has "possession" of collateral that's being held by someone who isn't the debtor (this also applies to a person who's leasing the collateral from a debtor as part of the debtor's ordinary course of business):

(1) When the person who actually has possession authenticates a record acknowledging they're holding the collateral for the secured party's benefit; or

(2) The person takes possession *after* authenticating a record acknowledging they're holding the collateral for the secured party's benefit.

(d) If perfection is dependent on possession of the collateral, then perfection only begins when the secured party takes possession and continues only while the secured party still has possession.

(e) Perfection of a security interest in a certificated security in registered form is perfected by delivery that meets 8–301's requirements and stays perfected by that delivery until the debtor gets possession of the security certificate.

(f) A person who has possession of collateral is not required to acknowledge it has possession for a secured party's benefit (*but see* (c)).

(g) If a person acknowledges it has possession for a secured party's benefit:

(1) the acknowledgement is effective under (c) or 8–301(a) even if it violates the debtor's rights; and

(2) unless the person agrees or some law other than Article Nine requires it, the person has no duty to the secured party to confirm the acknowledgement to anyone else.

(h) A secured party who has possession of collateral does not give up "possession" when it delivers the collateral to someone other than the debtor or someone who's leasing the collateral from the debtor in the ordinary course of the debtor's business if the person who gets delivery is instructed before or at the time of delivery:

(1) to keep possession for the secured party's benefit; or

(2) to redeliver the collateral to the secured party.

(i) A secured party does not give up "possession" even if a delivery under (h) violates the debtor's rights. A person who gets delivery of collateral under (h) has no duty to the secured party to confirm the delivery unless it agrees to do that, or some law other than Article Nine requires it.

9–314: PERFECTION BY CONTROL

(a) You may perfect your security interest in investment property, deposit accounts, letter-of-credit rights, electronic chattel paper or electronic documents by control under 7–106, 9–104, 9–105, 9–106, or 9–107.

(b) Perfection by control under 7–106, 9–104, 9–105, or 9–107 for deposit accounts, electronic chattel paper, letter-of-credit rights or electronic documents occurs only when the secured party gets control and lasts only so long as the secured party retains control.

(c) Perfection by control in investment property under 9–106 occurs from the time the secured party gets control and stays perfected until:

(1) the secured party loses control; and

(2) one of the following occurs:

(A) the debtor gets possession of the certificate, if the collateral is a certificated security (see 9–313(e));

(B) the issuer has registered or registers the debtor as the registered owner, if the collateral is an uncertificated security; or

(C) the debtor is or becomes the entitlement holder, if the collateral is a security entitlement.

9–315: WHAT HAPPENS UPON DISPOSITION OF COLLATERAL

(a) Except for wherever Article Nine or 2–403(2) is contrary to this general rule:

(1) a security interest or agricultural lien follows the collateral no matter how the collateral is disposed of (sale, exchange, trade, lease, etc.) unless the secured party agrees that the disposition may be made free of the security interest or agricultural lien; and

(2) a security interest automatically attaches to any identifiable proceeds of the collateral.

(b) Proceeds that get commingled with other property are still identifiable proceeds:

(1) if they're goods, to the extent provided by 9–336; and

(2) if they're not goods, to the extent that law and equitable principles outside of Article Nine allow tracing methods that identify the proceeds.

(c) As long as the security interest in the original collateral was perfected, a security interest in proceeds is automatically perfected subject to (d)'s rules.

(d) After 20 days from the time a security interest attaches to proceeds, perfection in those proceeds is lost unless:

(1) the following applies:

(A)–(C) If the proceeds aren't obtained with cash proceeds—if they are the result of barter or trade—and aren't described in the original financing statement, *but* they may be perfected by filing in the same original filing place, then perfection is continuous. This means that later records searchers must be on the lookout for property that was obtained by barter or trade, because it may be proceeds of some other secured party's collateral, and it could therefore be subject to a security interest that doesn't name that property—or even that category of collateral—in a UCC–1 filing naming the debtor;

(2) the proceeds are identifiable cash proceeds. In this case, perfection is continuous; or

(3) the security interest in the proceeds is perfected in some way other than automatically under (c) when the security interest attaches to the proceeds, or within 20 days of attachment.

Example: Secured party has an attached, perfected security interest in all of debtor's equipment and all of debtor's inventory, now held or hereafter acquired. Debtor sells a piece of equipment for cash, then uses those cash proceeds to buy inventory. Perfection in the inventory proceeds is continuous beyond the 20-day period because the original attached, perfected security interest already covers inventory.

Note: This subsection also states the obvious: if a secured party files an amendment specifically to perfect its interest in the proceeds during the 20-day grace period, then it's perfected in the proceeds before the end of the 20 days.

Note: Another way to look at this is that, by implication of (d)(1) and (d)(3), if proceeds are acquired with cash proceeds, the secured party must perfect within 20 days unless the proceeds acquired with cash proceeds are covered by the original security agreement and financing statement. However, (d)(3) is also satisfied if the secured party simply files an amendment to perfect its interest in proceeds.

(e) If a filed financing statement covers the original collateral, a security interest that is perfected due to (d)(1) becomes unperfected on the later occurrence of the following:

(1) when it would have lapsed due to the passage of time under 9–515 or is terminated under 9–513; or

(2) 21 days after the security interest attaches to the proceeds. This means that the secured party gets to take advantage of extra time after the usual lapse date if part of the 20-day grace period extends past the lapse date.

9–316: WHAT HAPPENS WHEN THE GOVERNING LAW CHANGES

(a) If a security interest has been properly perfected under 9–301(1) or 9–305(c), it stays perfected until whichever of these things happens first:

(1) perfection ends under the law of the correct jurisdiction;

(2) four months passes from the time the debtor moves to another jurisdiction; or

(3) one year passes from the time the debtor transfers the collateral to someone else who becomes the "debtor" and is located in another jurisdiction.

Note: The "one-year" rule of 9–316(a)(3) applies to collateral that is physically transferred from the original debtor to a transferee in a different jurisdiction in a way that makes the transferee a "debtor" under Article Nine because enforcement of the security interest isn't cut off (because, for example, the transfer is not an ordinary course of business sale). The one-year rule in (a)(3) allows more time for the secured party to track down the transferee and the collateral, which presumably will be more difficult when the transferee is in a different jurisdiction from the one where the secured party was used to dealing with the debtor.

(b) If a secured party perfects under the law of the new jurisdiction contemplated in (a) before time runs out, then perfection continues after the applicable (a) time runs out. But if the secured party doesn't perfect by the time it needs to under (a), then the security interest is treated as if it was *never* perfected against any "purchaser for value" of the collateral.*

(c) A security interest that is perfected by possession, except for certificate-of-title and as-extracted collateral goods, is continuously perfected if:

(1) the collateral is located in one jurisdiction while subject to a security interest perfected under the law of a different jurisdiction;

(2) the collateral is later brought into another jurisdiction; and

(3) once it's in the other jurisdiction it is perfected under the law of the other jurisdiction.

Note: Put differently, (c) says that if a secured party retains possession as collateral moves from one jurisdiction to another, perfection is continuous as long as the secured party follows the laws on what constitutes perfection by possession.

(d) Except for (e), if a security interest is properly perfected in another jurisdiction on goods for which this State requires a certificate of title, then the earlier perfection is still good until it would have ended under the laws of the other jurisdiction.

(e) A security interest in certificate-of-title goods covered by the situation in (d) becomes unperfected against a purchaser of the goods for value, including another secured party, if the perfection requirements under 9–311(b) (following the certificate-of-title laws, etc.) and 9–313 (perfection by possession, or in the case here, *re*possession) are not met by the time the earliest thing below occurs:

(1) the perfection would have ended anyway under the laws of the other jurisdiction even if a certificate of title wasn't issued here; or

(2) four months after the new certificate of title is issued in this state.

(f) A security interest in deposit accounts, letter-of-credit rights or investment property that is perfected under the law of the proper jurisdiction for the relevant bank, issuer, nominated person, or commodity intermediary (whichever applies) stays perfected until the earliest thing below happens:

(1) the perfection would have ended anyway under the law of that jurisdiction; or

(2) four months after the proper jurisdiction for perfection changes to another jurisdiction.

(g) If a secured party re-perfects in the new jurisdiction contemplated in (f) before the time periods run, then the original security interest stays perfected after the time periods run. In other words, there's continuous perfection. If a security interest is *not* re-perfected in the new jurisdiction before the time periods run, then it becomes *un*perfected, and the earlier perfection loses its effectiveness against any purchaser of the collateral for value.*

(h) When dealing with collateral that is *after-acquired during the four month grace period* after a debtor's location changes to another jurisdiction:

(1) A financing statement filed in the proper former jurisdiction under 9–301(1) or 9–305(c) before the debtor changed jurisdictions stays perfected in the after-acquired collateral as long as it would have been effective in the former jurisdiction if the debtor hadn't changed its jurisdictional location.

(2) If a secured party is perfected under (h)(1) and then perfects in the debtor's new jurisdiction before the expiration date of a financing statement in the former jurisdiction or within four months after the debtor changes locations, whichever happens first, the secured party stays continuously perfected after the four months in collateral the debtor acquired during the four-month grace period. If a security interest is *not* re-perfected in the new jurisdiction before the four-month grace period runs, then it becomes *un*perfected and the earlier perfection loses its effectiveness against any purchaser of the collateral for value.*

(i) If there is a "new debtor" situation, and there is a financing statement in the proper jurisdiction under 9–301(1) and 9–305(c) covering property of the original debtor, and the new debtor is located in a different jurisdiction:

(1) The financing statement stays effective in collateral existing before and for four months after the new debtor becomes bound under 9–203(d), if it still would have been effective against the original debtor in the proper jurisdiction for the original debtor.

(2) If a secured party re-perfects in the jurisdiction of the new debtor before the financing statement covering property of the original collateral becomes ineffective or before the end of the four-month grace period of (i)(2), then the original security interest stays perfected in the collateral of the new debtor after the grace period runs. In other words, there's continuous perfection. If a security interest is *not* re-perfected in the new jurisdiction before the time periods run, then it becomes *un*perfected and the earlier perfection loses its effectiveness against any purchaser of the collateral for value.*

* "Purchaser for value" includes even secured parties that a secured party might have had priority over before time ran out under (a), (f), (h), or (i), as applicable. Note also that lien creditors are not purchasers for value, so they don't get to jump ahead of a secured party whose perfection lapses under this subsection.

9–317: PRIORITY OF SECURITY INTEREST AND AGRICULTURAL LIEN V. ANOTHER INTEREST

(a) A security interest or agricultural lien is subordinate to:

(1) whoever gets priority over it under 9–322; and

(2) except for (e), a person who becomes a lien creditor before the earlier of (A) the security interest or agricultural lien becoming perfected; or (B) the time one of the conditions in 9–203(b)(3) for attachment is met and a financing statement is filed

Note: The (a)(2) rule is designed to protect secured parties when they have filed to perfect, thus giving public notice to later searchers, and when they also have obtained an authenticated security agreement from the debtor or have a possessory security interest. This allows for practical situations that may come about when, for example, the secured party has extended credit, has an enforceable security agreement and has filed to perfect regarding lending that will be used so the debtor may later obtain purchase money goods. In this situation, it wouldn't be fair for the secured party to lose out to an intervening party regarding the goods just because the debtor hadn't gotten rights in the goods at the time the later party's interest arose. Note also that in such a situation, this fills in the gap compared to the rule in (e) that provides a 20-day grace period for a purchase money secured party to file to perfect if they haven't already done so when the debtor gets possession of the purchase money goods.

(b) Except for (e), a buyer who isn't also a secured party of tangible chattel paper, tangible documents, goods, instruments or a security certificate takes free of a security interest or agricultural lien if the buyer gives value and receives delivery of the collateral before it knew of the security interest or agricultural lien and before it is perfected. Put differently, an innocent buyer beats an unperfected security interest.

(c) Except for (e), a lessee takes free of a security interest or agricultural lien if the lessee gives value and receives delivery of the collateral before it knows of the security interest or agricultural lien and before it is perfected. Put differently, an innocent lessee beats an unperfected security interest.

(d) A licensee of a general intangible or a buyer who isn't also a secured party of accounts, electronic chattel paper, electronic documents, general intangibles or investment property other than a certificated security takes free of a security interest if they give value before they knew of the security interest and before it is perfected. Put differently, all of these parties beat an unperfected security interest.

(e) Except for 9–320 and 9–321, if a purchase money secured party files to perfect within 20 days of the time the debtor receives delivery of the collateral, that security interest beats a buyer, lessee or lien creditor that gets its interest between the time the security interest attaches and the time of filing. This subsection makes clear there's a 20-day temporary perfection for purchase-money security interests that beats buyers, lessees and lien creditors that first come into the picture during the temporary perfection period.

9–318: WHAT HAPPENS WHEN THE DEBTOR SELLS AN ACCOUNT, CHATTEL PAPER, PAYMENT INTANGIBLE OR PROMISSORY NOTE

(a) Once a debtor sells an account, chattel paper, payment intangible or promissory note the debtor loses all rights in it. Remember that under Article Nine, for purposes of these kinds of sales the seller is the debtor and the buyer is the secured party.

(b) Until the buyer of an account or chattel paper perfects its "security interest," the debtor-seller still has the same rights to the collateral for purposes of determining the rights of other creditors or purchasers for value of the same account or chattel paper. In other words, those other parties may still claim their interests in the collateral up until the time the buyer perfects.

9–319: A CONSIGNEE'S RIGHTS AND TITLE V. THOSE OF OTHER PARTIES

(a) Except for (b), while a consignee has possession of goods, the consignee has the same rights and title to the goods as the consignor did, at least for purposes of figuring out the rights of the consignee's creditors or the rights of purchasers for value of the goods.

Note: This is how Article Nine consignors can lose priority to a consignee's creditors if the consignor doesn't take the 9–324(b) steps to protect its interests in the consigned goods.

(b) If something in Article Nine gives a perfected security interest of a consignor priority over a consignee's creditor, you can use non-Article Nine consignment laws to determine whatever rights remain for the non-Article Nine creditor.

9–320: WHEN BUYERS OF GOODS TAKE FREE OF SECURITY INTERESTS

(a) Except for (e), a buyer in the ordinary course of business that is not buying farm products from a farmer takes free of a security interest the buyer's seller created with the seller's creditor even if the security interest is perfected and the buyer knows about it.

Note: The Federal Food Security Act, 7 U.S.C. § 1631, preempts this subsection for most situations involving sales of farm products in the ordinary course of business. . .and reverses the usual Article Nine result.

(b) Except for (e), if someone buys someone else's consumer goods, the buyer takes free of a security interest the seller created with the seller's creditor, even if the security interest is perfected, as long as the buyer:

(1) doesn't know about the security interest;

(2) gives value in return for the goods;

(3) is buying primarily for their own consumer use; and

(4) buys before the seller's creditor filed a financing statement to perfect its interest in the consumer goods.

Note: This is sometimes called the garage sale rule because it would be applied in situations, such as a garage sale, where someone sells their consumer goods that are subject to a security interest to someone who also is going to use the goods as consumer goods. . .in other words, a consumer-to-consumer sale.

(c) The time periods in 9–316(a) and (b) control the effectiveness of perfection by filing when dealing with the priority of a security interest over the rights of a buyer under (b).

(d) A buyer in the ordinary course of business of minerals at the wellhead or minehead or after extraction takes free of an encumbrancer's interest.

(e) Security interests that are perfected by possession under 9–313 are not affected by (a) and (b).

9–321: LICENSEES AND LESSEES IN THE ORDINARY COURSE OF BUSINESS

(a) In this section, when we say "licensee in the ordinary course of business" we mean someone who becomes a licensee of a general intangible in good faith, not knowing the license violates someone else's rights in the thing licensed, and who gets the license from someone who's in the business of licensing those kinds of things. "Ordinary course of business" here means that the license is granted in a manner and is of the type that's usual (a) in the industry of which the licensor is a part or (b) in the licensor's own practices.

(b) A licensee in the ordinary course of business that gets a nonexclusive license takes free of any security interest the licensor created, even if the security interest is perfected and the licensee knows about it.

(c) A lessee in the ordinary course of business gets its lease rights free of any security interest the lessor created, even if the security interest is perfected and the lessee knows about it.

9–322: PRIORITY OF COMPETING SECURITY INTERESTS AND AGRICULTURAL LIENS

(a) Other than the exceptions in this section, here's how to rank the relative priorities of competing security interests and agricultural liens:

(1) Whoever filed or perfects first wins as between competing security interests and agricultural liens. To figure out what timing applies for priority-measuring purposes, assuming there's been no lapse of effectiveness of filing or perfection, use the earlier of the following:

(A) the time the filing is first made, or

(B) the time the security interest or agricultural lien is first perfected

Note: Remember that there can be a filing before there's perfection, so the secured party or agricultural lien holder gets the benefit of whichever timing measure works best for it.

(2) A perfected security interest or agricultural lien beats any competing security interest or agricultural lien that's unperfected.

(3) If neither of the competing interests is perfected, they rank in priority based on the time each attached.

(b) For purposes of (a)(1):

(1) use the time of filing or perfection regarding the original collateral as the time of filing or perfection of a security interest in proceeds. In other words, use the earlier time to measure priority instead of the later time when the proceeds come into being; and

(2) use the time of filing or perfection on the collateral that falls under Article Nine (see 9–203(g) and 9–308(d)) as the time of filing or perfection in any supporting obligation.

(c) Except for (f), if a security interest has priority under 9–327 (deposit accounts), 9–328 (investment property), 9–329 (letter-of-credit rights), 9–330 (chattel paper/instruments), or 9–331 (rights of purchasers of certain collateral under other Articles of the UCC), it also beats a security interest in:

(1) any supporting obligation for the collateral; and

(2) proceeds, if:

(A) the security interest in proceeds is perfected;

(B) the proceeds are cash proceeds or the same type of collateral as the original collateral; and

(C) in the case where there are proceeds of proceeds, all the proceeds that get generated in between are cash proceeds or proceeds that are the same type of collateral as the original collateral or are accounts generated by sale of the original collateral.

Note: If at some intervening point some proceeds that aren't these types are generated, (c)(2) won't apply.

(d) Except for (e) and (f), if a security interest in chattel paper, deposit accounts, negotiable documents, instruments, investment property or letter-of-credit rights was perfected by some method other than filing, then priorities between conflicting security interests in proceeds are determined by the time of each party's filing as to the proceeds. This means that whoever files first as to proceeds beats a competitor who hasn't filed, even if the non-filing competitor had perfected first with respect to the original collateral.

(e) Only apply (d) if the proceeds are not cash proceeds, chattel paper, deposit accounts, negotiable documents, instruments, investment property or letter-of-credit rights. Otherwise, go back to (a), (b) or (c) to figure out priority.

(f) Subsections (a) through (e) are subject to (g) and anything else in this section, as well as sections 4–201 (collecting bank's security interest), 5–118 (issuers and nominated persons) and 9–110 (security interests under sales in Article Two or leases in Article 2A).

(g) If the statute creating an agricultural lien says it has priority over other security interests or agricultural liens, apply that statute no matter what Article Nine says.

9–323: PRIORITY WITH RESPECT TO FUTURE ADVANCES

(a) Except for (c), if you're figuring out when perfection occurs for purposes of 9–322(a)(1), use the date an advance is made for security interests that serve as security *only* for advances that:

(1) are made while the security interest is perfected *only*:

(A) automatically under 9–309 when it attaches; or

(B) temporarily under 9–312(e)–(g); and

(2) are not made pursuant to a commitment made before or while the security interest was perfected in some way other than automatically or temporarily.

(b) Except for (c), a lien creditor beats a security interest that secures an advance made more than 45 days after the lien creditor gets its lien, unless the advance is made without knowing about the lien or the advance was a commitment to advance money that was entered into without knowing about the lien.

Note: This implies that a lien creditor loses out to a security interest protecting any advance made during the *first* 45 days after the lien creditor gets its lien. In other words, the secured party gets a free pass to priority on any advance made during the first 45 days after the lien creditor comes into the picture even if the secured party knew about the lien creditor. A secured party's advance *after* 45 days is protected against a lien creditor as long as the secured party didn't know at the time that the lien creditor existed.

(c) Don't apply (a) & (b) to a "security interest" of a buyer of accounts, chattel paper, payment intangibles or promissory notes, or of a consignor.

(d) Except for (e), a buyer of goods *not* in the ordinary course of business beats a security interest that secures an advance made after the secured party learns of the purchase or made 45 days after the purchase, whichever is first.

Note: This means that if a secured party advances money knowing that the collateral has been sold or makes its advance more than 45 days after the sale, the secured party loses to a non-ordinary course buyer. This makes sense because if the advance was made with knowledge of the sale or more than 45 days afterwards and the secured party hadn't checked on the status of the collateral, then the secured party must not have been concerned whether or not the collateral was still there.

(e) Don't apply (d) if the advance is made due to a commitment the secured party entered into without knowing of the purchase and before the 45-day period runs out.

(f) Except for (g), a lessee of goods *not* in the ordinary course of business takes its lease rights free of a security interest that secures advances made after whichever occurs first:

(1) the secured party learns of the lease; or

(2) 45 days after the lease contract becomes enforceable.

Note: Ditto comment from the note for (d), except here it applies to non-ordinary course lessees.

(g) Don't apply (f) if the advance is made due to a commitment the secured party entered into without knowing of the lease and before the 45-day period runs out.

9–324: SPECIAL PRIORITY FOR PURCHASE-MONEY SECURITY INTERESTS

(a) Except for (g), as long as it's perfected within 20 days of the time the debtor gets the collateral, a perfected purchase-money security interest in goods other than inventory or livestock beats any other security interest in the goods, including pre-existing floating lien security interests that covered the same category of goods, and, except for 9–327, a perfected security interest in the identifiable proceeds of the goods also has priority.

(b) Although you have to pay attention to (c) and (g), a perfected purchase-money security interest in *inventory* beats a conflicting security interest in the same inventory, including pre-existing floating lien security interests that covered the debtor's inventory, and beats a security interest in chattel paper or an instrument that is proceeds of the inventory and in proceeds of chattel paper (as long as 9–330 says so), and, except for exceptions in 9–327, it also has priority in identifiable cash proceeds that are received before or at the time the inventory is delivered to a buyer, *only if*:

(1) the purchase-money security interest is perfected when the debtor gets the inventory;

(2) the purchase-money secured party sends an authenticated notice to the conflicting security interest holder;

(3) the conflicting security interest holder receives the notice within five years before the debtor gets the inventory; and

(4) the notice says the sender has or expects to acquire a purchase-money security interest in the debtor's inventory and describes the inventory.

(c) The notice requirements of (b)(2)–(4) only apply to conflicting security interests with filed financing statements for the same type of inventory:

(1) if the competing secured party filed to perfect before the purchase-money secured party perfected by filing, or

(2) before the beginning of the purchase-money secured party's 20-day temporary perfection period under 9–312(f) if that applies.

Example: The rule in (c)(2) applies if the goods are held by a bailee on behalf of the secured party in situations such as a field warehouse where a document of title is issued but hasn't been delivered yet to the secured party.

(d) Except as (e) and (g) apply, a perfected purchase-money security interest in livestock that are farm products beats a conflicting security interest in the same livestock and, except for the exceptions in 9–317, a perfected security interest in their proceeds has priority in their proceeds and identifiable products in their unmanufactured states, *only if*:

(1) the purchase-money security interest is perfected when the debtor gets the livestock;

(2) the purchase-money secured party sends an authenticated notice to the conflicting security interest holder;

(3) the conflicting security interest holder receives the notice within five years before the debtor gets the livestock; and

(4) the notice says the sender has or expects to acquire a purchase-money security interest in the debtor's livestock and describes the livestock.

(e) The notice requirement of (d)(2)–(4) only applies to conflicting security interests that filed financing statements for the same type of livestock:

(1) if the competing secured party filed to perfect before the purchase-money secured party perfected by filing; or

(2) before the beginning of the purchase-money secured party's 20-day temporary perfection period under 9–312(f) if that applies.

Example: The rule in (e)(2) applies if the livestock are held by a bailee on behalf of the secured party.

(f) Except for (g), a perfected purchase-money security interest in software beats a conflicting security interest in the same collateral, and, except for exceptions in 9–327, a perfected security interest in its identifiable proceeds also has priority, at least so far as the purchase-money security interest in the goods the software is to be used with has priority in those goods and their proceeds under the general rules of this section—and it should have, if it meets the criteria to be a purchase-money security interest in software under 9–103(c).

(g) If there are multiple purchase-money security interests in the same collateral under (a), (b), (d) or (f):

(1) a purchase-money security interest of the *seller* of the collateral to the debtor beats a security interest of someone who gives value to help the debtor get the collateral; and

(2) in all other cases, apply 9–322(a)'s first-in-time rules.

9–325: PRIORITY IN TRANSFERRED COLLATERAL

(a) Except for (b), a security interest that a debtor creates in collateral is subordinate to a security interest another person created in the collateral if the debtor got the collateral subject to the other person's *already-perfected* security interest, and the other person's security interest stays perfected.

Example: Debtor grants a security interest in all of its equipment to Secured Party A. Debtor then sells a piece of its equipment to Buyer. Buyer had granted a floating lien security interest in Buyer's own equipment to Secured Party B. Secured Party A beats Secured Party B if Secured Party A perfected before the equipment was transferred to Buyer. This is true even if Secured Party B had perfected on its security interest with Buyer before Secured Party A had perfected on its security interest with Seller.

(b) Subsection (a) only subordinates a security interest if it:

(1) would have priority only under 9–322(a) or 9–324; or

(2) arose only under the special sale and lease "security interest" rules of 2–711(3) or 2A–508(5).

9–326: PRIORITY OF SECURITY INTERESTS CREATED IN A NEW DEBTOR'S PROPERTY

(a) Except for (b), a security interest created in the property of a "new debtor" that is perfected by a filed financing statement that is effective only because of 9–316(i) or 9–508 is beaten by a security interest that is perfected by some way other than the 9–316(i) or 9–508 rules.

Note: 9–316(i) and 9–508 are rules about temporary perfection when a "new debtor" assumes another's obligations. These rules cover how to turn that temporary perfection into continuous perfection.

Example: Until a new initial financing statement is filed naming the new debtor, the secured party with a security interest in the collateral transferred to that new debtor loses to a floating lien-perfected secured party in the new debtor's property that is the same category of collateral as the collateral that was transferred.

(b) Other parts of Article Nine sort out the priorities between security interests that are effective only under the 9–326(i) and 9–508 temporary and continuous perfection rules. In other words, you can just apply a first-in-time is first-in-right rule to these types of secured creditors who each have an interest in the same debtor's collateral and then, for example, have to deal with the merger of their shared debtor into a new debtor. However, if the new debtor is taking on obligations of a number of different debtors, then the security interests of the different debtors rank in priority against each other in the new debtor based on the order in which the new debtor bound itself, by agreement or operation of external law, to each security interest. This situation can arise in several ways—for example, there might be serial transactions occurring in which the new debtor company keeps merging with or acquiring the assets of a bunch of other companies.

Note: This implies that if two secured parties each have interests in the same collateral of a debtor, and that debtor merges into a new debtor, whichever secured party files first under the new debtor's name gets priority over the other secured party. This is so even if that secured party didn't have priority when the parties were just dealing with the original debtor. We have this result because the secured party who files is no longer relying on its 9–316(i) or 9–508 automatic and continuous perfection rights. Instead, it has elevated itself to become a new secured party of the new debtor.

9–327: PRIORITY OF SECURITY INTERESTS IN DEPOSIT ACCOUNTS

Here are the rules governing priority of security interests in deposit accounts:

(1) A security interest perfected by control under 9–104 beats a security interest that does not have control.

(2) Except for (3) and (4), security interests that have control rank according to the *time* they obtained control, as opposed to the *form* of control they have.

(3) Except for (4), a bank's security interest in a deposit account at that bank beats all other secured parties.

(4) A security interest that is perfected by control by the secured party becoming the bank's customer on the deposit account under 9–104(a)(3) beats even the bank's security interest under (3).

9–328: PRIORITY OF SECURITY INTERESTS IN INVESTMENT PROPERTY

Here are the rules governing priority of security interests in investment property:

(1) A security interest perfected by some type of control under 9–106 beats a security interest without control.

(2) Except for (3) and (4), security interests that each have control rank by time as follows:

(A) if the collateral is a security, the time the secured party got control;

(B) if the collateral is a security entitlement carried in a securities account and:

(i) if the secured party got control under 8–106(d)(1), then use the time they became the person for whom the account is maintained, or

(ii) if the secured party got control under 8–106(d)(2), then use the time of the security intermediary's agreement to follow the secured party's orders on the account, or

(iii) if the secured party got control through another person under 8–106(d)(3), use the time you'd use to figure priority under this paragraph if the other person were the secured party; or

(C) if the collateral is a commodity contract carried with a commodity intermediary, the time that requirements for control under 9–106(b)(2) are met.

(3) A securities intermediary's security interest in a securities entitlement or a securities account maintained with the intermediary beats all other security interests, even if the other interests arose before the intermediary's.

(4) A commodity intermediary's security interest in a commodity contract or a commodity account maintained with the intermediary beats all other security interests, even if the other interests arose before the intermediary's.

(5) A security interest in a certificated security in registered form perfected by taking delivery under 9–313(a) rather than control under 9–314 beats any other security interest that is *not* perfected by control.

(6) Conflicting security interests of a broker, securities intermediary or commodity intermediary rank equally if *none* are perfected by control.

(7) In all other cases, apply 9–322 and 9–323 to sort out priorities in investment property.

9–329: PRIORITY OF SECURITY INTERESTS IN LETTER-OF-CREDIT RIGHTS

Here are the rules governing priority of security interests in letter-of-credit rights:

(1) A security interest perfected by control under 9–107 beats, to the extent of its control, a security interest without control.

(2) Security interests perfected by control under 9–314 rank according to the time each got control.

Note: The only type of perfection without control allowed for letter-of-credit rights is when the letter-of-credit right was a supporting obligation for an account or other type of primary obligation.

9–330: PRIORITY OF PURCHASERS OF CHATTEL PAPER OR INSTRUMENTS

(a) Someone who purchases chattel paper, including a secured party, beats a security interest in the chattel paper that exists only because the chattel paper is proceeds of inventory if:

(1) in good faith in the ordinary course of the purchaser's business, the purchaser gives new value and gets possession or control of the chattel paper under 9–105; and

(2) the chattel paper has not been stamped or written on to identify a secured party it's already been assigned to and who is not the purchaser.

(b) Someone who purchases chattel paper beats a security interest in the chattel paper that is claimed as *more than just proceeds* of inventory if the purchaser gives new value and gets possession or control in good faith under 9–105 in the ordinary course of its business without knowing the purchase violates the secured party's rights.

(c) Except for 9–327, a purchaser who gets priority in chattel paper under (a) or (b) gets priority in chattel paper proceeds to the extent:

(1) 9–322 grants priority; or

(2) the proceeds are the specific goods covered by the chattel paper or are cash proceeds of the specific goods, *even if* the purchaser's security interest is unperfected.

Example: Goods were sold on credit, and the sale generated chattel paper. The seller had a pre-existing loan from Bank A that took a floating lien security interest in the seller's inventory. The seller used the chattel paper to secure a loan it took from Bank B, which therefore became the "purchaser" of the chattel paper. Then, the goods were repossessed or sold for cash after the original sale, because the account debtor defaulted on its payment obligations under the chattel paper. In this scenario, Bank B has priority over the proceeds, regardless of whether you view the proceeds as the repossessed goods or the cash received from re-sale.

(d) Except for 9–331(a), a purchaser of an instrument beats a security interest that is perfected by something other than possession if the purchaser gives value and takes possession of the instrument in good faith without knowing the purchase violates the secured party's rights.

(e) When dealing with (a) and (b), a purchase-money secured creditor in inventory is considered to have given new value for chattel paper that is proceeds of the inventory.

(f) When dealing with (b) and (d), if chattel paper or an instrument is stamped, written on, or otherwise identifies a secured party who it's been assigned to and who is not the purchaser, then the purchaser has knowledge that the purchase violates the secured party's rights. This is true even if the notice of the secured party's identity *doesn't* say something like, "Any transfer of this chattel paper is void unless we agree to it."

9–331: LIMITATIONS OF ARTICLE NINE WITH RESPECT TO NEGOTIABLE INSTRUMENTS, NEGOTIABLE DOCUMENTS, AND INVESTMENT SECURITIES

(a) Article Nine does not change the rights of a holder in due course of a negotiable instrument, a holder to whom a negotiable document has been duly negotiated, or a protected purchaser of a security. If Articles Three, Seven, or Eight say so, these parties beat even earlier perfected security interests.

(b) Article Nine doesn't affect the protections from claims that Article Eight gives regarding investment securities.

(c) An Article Nine filing is not a notice of claim or defense to the parties in (a) and (b).

9–332: TRANSFER OF MONEY OR FUNDS FROM A DEPOSIT ACCOUNT

(a) As long as someone who receives a transfer of money does not collude with the debtor in violating a secured party's rights, the transferee beats the secured party.

(b) As long as someone who gets funds from a deposit account does not collude with the debtor in violating a secured party's rights, the transferee beats the secured party.

9–333: PRIORITY OF POSSESSORY LIENS

(a) A "possessory lien" means an interest that *isn't* a security interest or agricultural lien:

(1) that acts as security for payment for services or materials a person provided in the ordinary course of their business in connection with goods;

(2) that is created by a statute or common law in favor of the person; and

(3) that is only effective if the person has possession of the goods.

(b) A possessory lien beats a security interest unless the lien is statutory and the statute says it doesn't.

9–334: FIXTURES

(a) An Article Nine security interest may be created in fixtures or may continue in goods that become fixtures, even if the goods weren't originally fixtures. Fixtures don't include ordinary building materials.

Example: A water heater for someone's home is a consumer good when purchased at a store but becomes a fixture when installed at the home.

Example: Lumber used to frame a house is an ordinary building material and not a fixture.

(b) Article Nine doesn't prevent real estate law from having its own set of effective rules to create an encumbrance on fixtures.

(c) Where (d) and (h) don't apply, the general rule is that a security interest in fixtures is lower in priority to an owner or encumbrancer of the real estate that has a conflicting interest. This is true as long as the owner/encumbrancer is not also the debtor. It wouldn't make sense for a defaulting debtor to have priority over its secured party!

(d) Except for (h), which deals with construction mortgages, a perfected purchase money security interest in fixtures beats the interest of an encumbrancer or owner if the debtor has an interest shown in the real estate records or is in possession of the real estate (for example, as a tenant), and:

(1) the security interest is in fact a purchase money security interest;

(2) the interest of the encumbrancer or owner existed before the goods became fixtures; and

(3) the security interest is perfected by a fixture filing before the time the goods become fixtures, or within 20 days after they become fixtures.

(e) A perfected security interest in fixtures beats an owner or encumbrancer and even the superpriority of a construction mortgage under (h) if:

(1) the debtor has an interest shown in the real estate records or is in possession of the real property (for example, as a tenant), and the security interest:

(A) is perfected by a fixture filing before the encumbrancer or owner gets its interest on the real estate records; and

(B) has priority over any conflicting interest of someone who owned or encumbered the real estate before the current owner or encumbrancer;

Note: In other words, if you have a fixture-filed security interest, you beat an owner or encumbrancer that comes along *after* you so long as you also could have beaten the owners or encumbrancers who were around *before* the new ones showed up.

(2) the security interest in the goods is perfected by any Article Nine method before they became fixtures and are readily removable:

(A) factory or office machines;

(B) equipment that isn't primarily used or leased to operate the real estate; or

Example: Desktop computers that are programmed to control temperatures in an apartment building are an example of equipment primarily used or leased to operate the real estate (apartment).

(C) replacements of domestic appliances that are consumer goods;

Example: A refrigerator that a tenant buys and has installed in their apartment to replace the original refrigerator that the building owner installed in the apartment is an example of a replacement of a domestic appliance (refrigerator).

(3) the conflicting security interest is a real property lien obtained through a court proceeding after the security interest was perfected by *any* Article Nine method; or

(4) the security interest is in a manufactured-home transaction and is perfected under a statute of the type specified in 9–311(a)(2).

(f) Whether or not it's perfected, a security interest in fixtures beats an owner or encumbrancer if:

(1) the owner or encumbrancer in an authenticated record agrees to subordinate or otherwise not assert an interest in the goods as fixtures; or

(2) the debtor has the legal right to remove the goods despite the interest of the owner or encumbrancer.

(g) The priority of the security interest in (f)(2) continues for a reasonable time if the debtor loses its right to remove the goods despite the owner's or encumbrancer's interest.

(h) A "construction mortgage" is one that secures an obligation for construction of an improvement on land, including the cost of buying the land, if the mortgage says it is one. Examples of an improvement on land are original construction or a renovation. Except for (e) and (f), a construction mortgage beats a security interest in fixtures if it's recorded in the real estate records office before the goods become fixtures *and the goods become fixtures before construction is completed.* The construction mortgage keeps its priority even if there is a later refinancing of the debt in the property.

Note: This all means that the construction mortgage gets a superpriority even over purchase money security interests for fixtures installed during construction, but it doesn't get that superpriority over PMSI secured parties who come into the picture after construction. Furthermore, the superpriority status isn't lost if there's a later refinance by the debtor and the original construction mortgage is no longer in place.

(i) A perfected security interest in crops growing on real estate beats an owner or encumbrancer if the debtor has an interest shown on the real estate records or is in possession of the real estate (for example, as a tenant).

(j) Subsection (i) supersedes any inconsistent provisions in the following statutes: [the State legislature lists the jurisdiction's statutes that should apply here].

9–335: SECURITY INTERESTS IN ACCESSIONS

(a) You may create a security interest in an accession, and an earlier security interest in something that became an accession stays with the thing when it becomes an accession.

(b) If a security interest is perfected when something becomes an accession, then it stays perfected after the thing becomes an accession.

(c) Except for (d), use Article Nine's regular priority rules to figure out priorities in an accession.

Note: This means, for example, that assuming application of the 9–322(a) first-to-file-or-perfect rule, whoever filed first gets priority in the accession specifically, or even the whole item the accession is combined with, if the security agreement and filing indicate that is what is intended. In the same way, a purchase-money security interest in an accession takes priority over a prior security interest in the whole item the accession is combined with.

(d) A security interest in the whole item the accession is combined with beats a security interest in the accession if the interest in the whole item is perfected under a certificate-of-title law.

(e) If the debtor defaults, the secured party may use the 9–600s procedures to remove the accession from the item it is combined with if it has priority over everyone else who has an interest in the whole item.

(f) If removing the accession causes any physical damage to the whole or to other things, the removing secured party has to reimburse anyone else who has an interest in the whole (other than the debtor) for the cost of repairing the damaged stuff. The removing secured party doesn't need to reimburse a holder or owner for a reduction in the value of the whole or to other things where the reduction is caused by the removal. Someone who *is* entitled to reimbursement may refuse permission for removal until there is adequate assurance the reimbursement will be made. Adequate assurance could take the form of establishment of an escrow account in the amount of anticipated damage.

9–336: SECURITY INTERESTS IN COMMINGLED GOODS

(a) "Commingled goods" are things that are combined with other things in a way that causes them to lose their separate identities as together they become something else.

Example: Eggs, butter and sugar combined together to create a cake are commingled goods.

(b) There is no security interest in commingled goods because by definition they can't be separated out from other things. Instead there is only a security interest that may attach to the product or mass that is the result of the commingling.

(c) If collateral that had a security interest attached to it becomes commingled goods, then the security interest attaches to the product or mass that results.

Example: An attached security interest in eggs that become part of a cake results in the egg-attached security interest changing into a security interest in the cake.

(d) Perfection of a security interest in collateral before it gets commingled creates perfection in the product or mass that results if the collateral is commingled.

Example: A perfected security in eggs that become part of a cake results in the egg-perfected security interest changing into a perfected security interest in the cake.

(e) Except for (f), use Article Nine's regular priority rules to figure out the priorities in the product or mass that results from commingled goods.

Note: In these situations, a prior-perfected security interest in the final product beats a later-perfected security interest in one of the commingled goods. Likewise, a prior-perfected security interest in commingled goods beats a security interest in the final product that was perfected after the commingled goods security interest was perfected.

(f) If more than one security interest attaches to the product or mass because of (c), use the following priority rules:

(1) Security interests that are perfected under (d) beat security interests that were unperfected when the goods were commingled.

(2) If two or more security interests are perfected under (d), rank them equally by their proportion to each other compared to the value of the product or mass that results from the commingling.

Note: The rule in (f)(2) means that the first-to-file-or-perfect rule does not apply in this situation. Instead, the perfected security interests are ranked equally in terms of priority, and there is only a division of value relative to each other and the finished product.

Example: Secured Party A has a security interest in $300 worth of eggs used to bake a cake. Secured Party B has a security interest in $500 worth of sugar used to bake the same cake. To figure out priority, first determine the value of the cake. 3/8th of that value is credited to the eggs, and 5/8ths of that value is credited to the sugar. If the resulting dollar amount is more than what is owed to either of the secured parties, the overage goes back into the pot for other creditors.

9–337: PRIORITY IN GOODS COVERED BY A CERTIFICATE OF TITLE

If this State issues a clean certificate of title that does not show a specific security interest attaches to the goods, and the certificate is issued on goods where a security interest is perfected in any way in another jurisdiction by, for example, notation on a certificate of title issued in that other jurisdiction, then:

(1) someone who buys the goods but isn't in the business of selling those kinds of goods beats the secured party whose interest should have been shown on the clean certificate, so long as the buyer gives value and gets delivery of the goods after the clean certificate is issued and without knowing about the security interest that should have been noted on the clean certificate; and

(2) a later secured party that perfects its interest under 9–311(b) beats the earlier secured party whose interest should have been noted on the clean certificate if the later secured party got its interest after the clean certificate was issued and before it knew about the earlier security interest.

9–338: WHAT HAPPENS IF A SECURITY INTEREST OR AGRICULTURAL LIEN IS PERFECTED BY A FILING THAT PROVIDES INCORRECT INFORMATION

If a security interest or agricultural lien is perfected by a filing that incorrectly provides information required in 9–516(b)(5), it loses priority to:

(1) a conflicting security interest to the extent that the competitor reasonably relied on the incorrect information when it gave value; and

(2) a purchaser, other than a secured party, that reasonably relied on the incorrect information when it gave value or when it received delivery of tangible chattel paper, tangible documents, goods, instruments or a security certificate as collateral.

9–339: PRIORITY CAN BE VOLUNTARILY SUBORDINATED

Anyone who has priority under Article Nine is free to subordinate their priority position to someone else, such as to a secured party holding a conflicting security interest.

9–340: BANK'S SET-OFF OR RECOUPMENT RIGHTS

(a) Except for (c), a bank may exercise its set-off or recoupment rights against a customer's deposit account even if a secured party has a security interest in that deposit account.

(b) Except for (c), a bank keeps its set-off and recoupment rights in a customer's account even if the bank is also a secured party in the deposit account.

(c) If a secured party has control of a deposit account by getting named as a customer on that deposit account under 9–104(a)(3), the bank's set-off and recoupment rights aren't effective against the secured party.

9–341: BANK'S RIGHTS AND DUTIES REGARDING A DEPOSIT ACCOUNT

Except for 9–340(c) or if the bank agrees in an authenticated record, the bank's rights and duties regarding a deposit account are not affected if a security interest is created, attached or perfected in the deposit account, even if the bank knows about the security interest, or even if the bank receives instructions from the secured party.

9–342: BANK'S RIGHTS WITH RESPECT TO A CONTROL AGREEMENT

A bank doesn't have to enter into an agreement under 9–104(a) to follow a secured party's instructions even if its customer tells it to do so. If a bank does enter into that kind of agreement, it doesn't have to confirm the existence of the agreement to anyone else unless the customer asks it to do so.

INTRODUCTION TO THE 9–400s

The 9–400s ("Part 4" of Article Nine) discuss the rights of third parties, including contract counterparties, assignees, account debtors, lessors, lessees, and others who may come into contact or have transactions with Article Nine debtors and secured parties.

9–401: A DEBTOR'S ABILITY TO TRANSFER RIGHTS IN COLLATERAL

(a) Laws other than Article Nine tell you whether or not a debtor's rights in collateral may be voluntarily or involuntarily transferred, except for (b) and 9–406, 9–407, 9–408 and 9–409.

(b) A debtor's rights can still be transferred even if the debtor and secured party agree that (1) the debtor can't transfer those rights or (2) the transfer would constitute a default by the debtor.

9–402: SECURED PARTY'S LIABILITY FOR DEBTOR'S ACTIONS

A secured party is not liable in contract or tort for bad things the debtor does just because the secured party happens to have a security interest in the debtor's collateral.

9–403: AGREEMENT BETWEEN ACCOUNT DEBTOR AND ASSIGNOR

(a) In this section, "value" has the same meaning as in 3–303(a).

(b) Except where we say otherwise, if an account debtor and an assignor agree not to assert against an assignee any claim or defense the account debtor may have against the assignor, that agreement is enforceable if the assignee takes the assignment for value, in good faith, without knowing of a claim or possessory right in whatever was assigned and without knowing about a defense or claim in recoupment that a person may have in connection with a negotiable instrument under 3–305(a).

(c) Don't apply (b) to defenses that may be made against a holder in due course of a negotiable instrument under 3–305(b).

(d) In a consumer transaction, even if the consumer's agreement to pay doesn't have statements in it that may be required under consumer laws to say that the consumer (who is usually the account debtor) has the right to make any defense or claim against an assignee that it could make against the original creditor (the original obligee), then the agreement should be treated as if it *did* have the required statements, and the consumer account debtor may assert defenses or claims against the assignee just as if the statements were included.

(e) If there is another law outside of Article Nine that sets different rules for individual account debtors in consumer transactions, then apply that law.

(f) Except for (d), this section doesn't change any law other than one in Article Nine that would allow enforcement of an agreement by an account debtor not to make defenses or claims against an assignee.

9–404: ASSIGNEE'S RIGHTS AND LIMITATIONS

(a) Unless an account debtor agreed not to assert against an assignee any defense or claim it may have, the assignee's rights are subject to:

(1) any terms of the agreement between the account debtor and the assignor, and also any defense or claim of recoupment the account debtor may have from the transaction that created the account; and

(2) any other defense or claim the account debtor might have that arose before the account debtor got an authenticated notice that the account had been assigned.

(b) Except for (c) and (d), an account debtor's claim against the assignor may only be used against an assignee under (a) to reduce the amount owed to the assignee.

(c) If there is another law outside of Article Nine that sets different rules for individual account debtors in consumer transactions, then apply that law.

(d) Some laws require that in a consumer transaction there must be a record of how much the account debtor owes and a statement that says the account debtor's recovery against an assignee may not be more than what is to be paid according to that record. If the record doesn't contain that legally-required statement, the account debtor's right to recover from an assignee is treated as if the record *did* contain the statement.

(e) This section doesn't apply to an assignment of a health-care-receivable.

9–405: MODIFICATION OF AN ASSIGNED CONTRACT

(a) If an account debtor and an assignor change or substitute an assigned contract in good faith, that action is binding on the assignee. The assignee also gets whatever rights are due to it under the changed or substituted contract. However, the assignment may say that modification or substitution is a breach of contract by the assignor. These rules are subject to (b) through (d).

(b) The rules of (a) apply to the extent that

(1) there is still some performance required in all or in part under the assigned contract before the right to payment is final; or

(2) the assignor has fully performed and the account debtor has not yet received notification of assignment under 9–406(a).

(c) If there is another law outside of Article Nine that sets different rules for individual account debtors in consumer transactions, then apply that law.

(d) This section doesn't apply to an assignment of a health-care-receivable.

9–406: ASSIGNMENTS AND ACCOUNT DEBTORS

(a) Except for (b) through (i), if an account debtor on an account, chattel paper or payment intangible pays off the obligation to an assignor before receiving an authenticated notice of assignment that says payment should be made to the assignee, then treat the payment as if it was made to the assignee. However, once it gets notice, the account debtor must pay the assignee to discharge the obligation.

(b) Except for (h), notification under (a) is ineffective:

(1) if it doesn't reasonably identify what rights are assigned;

(2) to the extent an agreement is effective under law between the account debtor and the *seller* of a payment intangible that limits the account debtor's duty to pay someone other than the seller; or

(3) at the account debtor's option if the notification tells the account debtor to make only partial payment to the assignee, even if

(A) only a portion of the account, chattel paper or payment intangible is assigned to the assignee;

(B) a portion is assigned to a different assignee; or

(C) the account debtor knows the assignee took only a limited assignment.

(c) Except for (h), if the account debtor asks for it, an assignee must seasonably provide reasonable proof of the assignment. If the assignee doesn't comply, the account debtor may pay the assignor to discharge its obligation, even if it has notice under (a).

(d) Except for (e), (h) and (k), and 2A–303 and 9–407, *an agreement* between an account debtor and an assignor or in a promissory note is ineffective to the extent that it:

(1) prohibits, restricts or requires the account debtor's or promissory note obligor's consent to creation, assignment, transfer or any other activity regarding a security interest in the account, chattel paper, payment intangible or promissory note; or

(2) provides that doing anything in connection with a security interest, including creating or enforcing one, gives rise to default, breach, right of recoupment, claim, defense termination, right of termination, or remedy under the account, chattel paper, payment intangible, or promissory note.

(e) Don't apply (d) to the *sale* of a payment intangible or promissory note unless the sale is part of a 9–610 disposition or a 9–620 acceptance of collateral.

(f) Except for (h), (i) and (k) and 2A–303 and 9–407, *operation of law by statute or otherwise* that interferes with or requires the consent of a governmental body or official or account debtor to doing anything in connection with a security interest, including creating or enforcing one, in an account or chattel paper is ineffective, and it also is ineffective if it provides that doing anything in connection with a security interest, including creating or enforcing one, gives rise to default, breach, right of recoupment, claim, defense termination, right of termination, or remedy under the account or chattel paper.

(g) Except for (h), an account debtor's waiver or variation of its option under (b)(3) is ineffective.

(h) If there is another law outside of Article Nine that sets different rules for individual account debtors in consumer transactions, then apply that law.

(i) This section doesn't apply to a health-care-insurance receivable.

(j) [If the state legislature hasn't amended its statutes, rules and regulations to conform to the requirements of this section, then list the things that are inconsistent here.]

(k) Don't apply (d), (f) and (j) to security interests in an ownership interest in a general partnership, a limited partnership or a limited liability company.

9–407: RESTRICTIONS REGARDING LEASES OF GOODS

(a) Except for (b), a term in a lease of goods is *ineffective* if it:

(1) prevents assigning, transferring, or creating, attaching, perfecting or enforcing a security interest a party has under the lease contract or in the lessor's residual interest in the leased goods; or

(2) says that assigning, transferring, or creating, attaching, perfecting or enforcing a security interest gives rise to default, breach, right of recoupment, claim, defense termination, right of termination, or remedy under the lease.

(b) Except for 2A–303(7), a term of the type described in (a)(2) is *effective* to the extent:

(1) a lessee transfers its right to possess or use the goods in violation of the term; or

(2) a party delegates material performance of its obligations under the lease to someone in violation of the term.

(c) Creating, attaching, perfecting or enforcing a security interest in the lessor's interest under the lease contract is not the type of transfer that damages a lessee's interest under the lease for purposes of 2A–303(4), unless, and only to the extent that, enforcing the security interest actually leads to delegation to someone else of the lessor's obligation of material performance.

9–408: INEFFECTIVE RESTRICTIONS ON CERTAIN ASSIGNMENTS

(a) Except for (b), any term in a promissory note or agreement between an account debtor and a debtor relating to a health-care-insurance receivable or a general intangible, including a contract, permit, license or franchise, that prohibits, restricts or requires consent of a party before assigning, transferring, or creating, attaching, perfecting or enforcing a security interest in the note or agreement is ineffective if it:

(1) would hinder creation, attachment or perfection of the security interest; or

(2) makes assigning, transferring, or creating, attaching, perfecting or enforcing a security interest a default, breach, right of recoupment, claim, defense termination, right of termination, or remedy under the promissory note, health-care-insurance receivable or general intangible.

(b) Subsection (a) applies only to *sales* of payment intangibles or promissory notes unless the sale is part of a **9–610** disposition or a **9–620** acceptance of collateral.

(c) Except for (f), *operation of law by statute or otherwise* that interferes with or requires the consent of a governmental body or official or account debtor to do anything in connection with a security interest, including creating or enforcing one, in a promissory note, health-care-insurance receivable or general intangible, including a contract, permit, license or franchise, is ineffective, and it also is ineffective if it provides that doing anything in connection with a security interest, including creating or enforcing one, gives rise to default, breach, right of recoupment, claim, defense termination, right of termination, or remedy under the promissory note, health-care-insurance receivable or general intangible.

Note: Subsections (a) and (c) don't override agreement terms or laws that might as a practical matter hinder assignment of one of the types of property described here. Instead, they only override terms that *prohibit, restrict or require consent* to the assignment.

(d) If there is a term in a promissory note or an agreement between an account debtor and a debtor relating to a health-care-insurance receivable or a general intangible or a rule of law overridden by (a) or (c) that *would be* effective under a rule of law outside of Article Nine but *would not* be effective under (a) or (c), then creating, attaching or perfecting a security interest in the note or agreement:

(1) is not enforceable against the person obligated on the note or the account debtor;

(2) does not impose a duty or obligation on such a person;

(3) does not require such a person to recognize the security interest or act under it or accept payment or performance from the secured party;

(4) does not entitle the secured party to use or assign the debtor's rights under those things or any materials or information related to the transaction that gave rise to those things;

(5) does not entitle the secured party to access or use any trade secrets or confidential information of the person obligated on the promissory note or the account debtor; and

(6) does not entitle the secured party to enforce the security interest in the promissory note or health-care-insurance receivable or general intangible.

Note: Subsection (d) makes (a) and (c) inapplicable against account debtors on general intangibles and health-care insurance receivables, as well as persons obligated on promissory notes, if other rules restrict the effectiveness of an assignment or the ability to exercise remedies.

(e) [If the state legislature hasn't amended its statutes, rules and regulations to conform to the requirements of this section, then list the things that are inconsistent here.]

(f) Don't apply this section to security interests in an ownership interest in a general partnership, a limited partnership or a limited liability company.

9–409: INEFFECTIVE RESTRICTIONS ON ASSIGNMENT OF LETTER-OF-CREDIT RIGHTS

(a) A term in or law applying to a letter of credit that prohibits, restricts or requires the consent of an applicant, issuer or nominated person to a beneficiary's assignment or creation of an interest in a letter-of-credit right is ineffective if it:

(1) impairs creation, attachment or perfection regarding a security interest in the letter-of-credit right; or

(2) provides that an action involving creation or other activity regarding a security interest in the letter-of-credit right is a default, breach, right of recoupment, claim, defense termination, right of termination, or remedy under the letter-of-credit right.

(b) If a term in a letter-of-credit is ineffective under (a) but *would* be effective under law outside of Article Nine or under the customs or practices involving letters-of-credit to the transfer of a right to draw or demand performance or to assign the right to proceeds under the letter of credit, then creating, attaching or perfecting a security interest in the letter-of-credit right:

(1) may not be enforced against the applicant, issuer, nominated person or transferee beneficiary;

(2) doesn't give rise to duties or obligations on the part of those parties; and

(3) doesn't require those parties to recognize the security interest or to render or accept payment or other performance from the secured party.

INTRODUCTION TO THE 9–500s

The 9–500s ("Part 5" of Article Nine) deals with the nitty-gritty of filing. Here you'll find provisions on how exactly to file a financing statement, the workings of the filing office that receives and indexes the financing statement, and information about what to do if there is a mistake in a financing statement.

9–501: THE FILING OFFICE

(a) Except for (b), if this is the jurisdiction whose law governs perfection of a security interest or agricultural lien, then file in:

(1) the office where you'd record a mortgage on real property if the collateral is as-extracted collateral or timber to be cut, or if you're filing on things that are, or will become, fixtures (so you want to do a fixture filing); or

(2) the office of [Legislature designates the filing office] in any other case, including if you're filing on things that are, or will become, fixtures, but you're *not* doing a fixture filing.

(b) File in the office of [Legislature designates the filing office] if you're perfecting a security interest in collateral, including fixtures, of a transmitting utility. The financing statement for these kinds of filings also serves as a fixture filing on the things indicated in the financing statement that are, or will become, fixtures.

Note: In many states, the filing office designated by the legislature is the office of the (state) Secretary of State.

9–502: WHAT TO INCLUDE IN A FINANCING STATEMENT

(a) Except for (b), a financing statement is sufficient only if it:

(1) provides the debtor's name (see 9–503);

(2) provides the secured party's name or their representative's name; and

(3) indicates the collateral covered by the financing statement (see 9–504).

(b) Except for 9–501(b), if your financing statement covers as-extracted collateral or timber to be cut, or is a fixture filing, you need to include everything in (a), plus you have to:

(1) indicate that's the type of collateral covered (for example: fixtures);

(2) indicate it's to be filed or, if dealing with a fixture filing, recorded, in the real property records;

(3) describe the real property it relates to in the same way a recorded real estate mortgage would describe the property, such as a metes and bounds description;

(4) include the name of a record owner of the property if the debtor doesn't have a record interest in the real estate. For example, if it's a fixture a renter is installing in a property owned by someone else, you'd include the name of the owner.

(c) For fixtures or as-extracted collateral or timber to be cut, a recorded mortgage, even if it's not an Article Nine fixture filing, is still effective as if it *is* a fixture filing from the date of recording *only if*:

(1) the recording indicates the goods or accounts it covers;

(2) the goods are, or will become, fixtures or are as-extracted collateral or timber to be cut related to the property in the record;

(3) the recording has the same types of content required under (b), although you don't need to say it should be filed in the real property records office because it already is; and

(4) the record is duly recorded.

(d) You may file a financing statement before a security agreement is made or a security interest attaches.

9–503 ALT A: HOW TO IDENTIFY THE DEBTOR AND THE SECURED PARTY

(a) A financing statement sufficiently provides the debtor's name:

(1) if the debtor is a registered organization or if the collateral is held in a trust that is a registered organization, then only if it provides the debtor's name as it currently appears on the public record **the registered organization filed in** ~~of~~ the jurisdiction where the debtor is organized;

(2) if the debtor is a decedent's estate, then only if it provides the name of the debtor and decedent and says a personal representative is dealing with the collateral;

(3) if the debtor is a trust or a trustee that is not a registered organization, then only if it:

(A) (i) provides the trust's name as shown in the document that formed the trust or (ii) if there's no specific name, then if it provides the name of the settlor or testator; and

(B) in another part of the financing statement (i) states that the collateral is held in a trust (if the name is provided under (A)(i)), or (ii) provides enough information so you can tell which trust it is if the same settlor or testator is on other trusts (if the name is provided under (A)(ii)) and indicates that the collateral is part of a trust;

Alternative A

(4) when dealing with an individual, except for (g), *only* if you use the debtor's name as it appears on an unexpired driver's license issued by this State;

(5) if (a)(4) doesn't apply to the individual, only if the financing statement uses the debtor's individual name or the debtor's surname and first personal name; and

(6) in situations where none of the above applies, if it uses:

(A) *only* the organizational name of the debtor if the debtor has a name; or

Example: Use the official name of a partnership.

(B) if the debtor has no name, *only* if it provides the names of each partner, member, associate and other person that comprise the debtor in a way that would be sufficient if the person was the debtor.

Example: If a partnership is so loosely organized that it doesn't use a name, then provide the names of each partner as described.

(b) A financing statement that provides the name of the debtor under (a) is not ineffective simply because it lacks:

(1) a trade name or other name of the debtor; or

(2) the names of each partner, member, associate or person that comprise the debtor, unless those names are required under (a)(6).

End of Alternative A

(c) It's not sufficient if the financing statement only provides the trade name of the debtor.

Example: If an individual owns a sole proprietorship that operates the business under a name that differs from the individual's, it would not be sufficient to use *only* the business name. Instead, you should make sure the name of the individual owner is used on the financing statement.

(d) A financing statement is not insufficient just because it doesn't indicate that the secured party or a representative of the secured party are acting in a representative capacity for another person.

(e) You may put multiple debtors and secured parties onto one financing statement. Of course, this assumes that the parties all relate to a single relationship that the financing statement involves. This provision just means that there's no need to file a new financing statement for each additional debtor or secured party in the same transaction.

(f) For purposes of indicating the "name of the decedent" under (a)(2), use the decedent's name as shown on the order appointing the personal representative that was issued by the court having jurisdiction over the collateral.

Alternative A

(g) Use the most recently issued driver's license if there is more than one that fits the description in (a)(4).

End of Alternative A

(h) "The "name of the settlor or testator" means:

(1) if the settlor or testator is a registered organization, the debtor's name as it currently appears on the public record of the jurisdiction where the debtor is organized; or

(2) in other cases, the name of the settlor or testator as shown in the document that formed the trust.

9–503 ALT B: HOW TO IDENTIFY THE DEBTOR AND THE SECURED PARTY

(a) A financing statement sufficiently provides the debtor's name:

(1) if the debtor is a registered organization or if the collateral is held in a trust that is a registered organization, then only if it provides the debtor's name as it currently appears on the public record **the registered organization filed in** ~~of~~ the jurisdiction where the debtor is organized;

(2) if the debtor is a decedent's estate, then only if it provides the name of the debtor and decedent and says a personal representative is dealing with the collateral;

(3) if the debtor is a trust or a trustee that is not a registered organization, then only if it:

(A) (i) provides the trust's name as shown in the document that formed the trust or (ii) if there's no specific name, then if it provides the name of the settlor or testator; and

(B) in another part of the financing statement (i) states that the collateral is held in a trust (if the name is provided under (A)(i)), or (ii) provides enough information so you can tell which trust it is if the same settlor or testator is on other trusts (if the name is provided under (A)(ii)) and indicates that the collateral is part of a trust;

Alternative B

(4) when dealing with an individual, *only* if you use:

(A) the debtor's individual name;

(B) the individual's surname and first personal name; or

(C) except for (g), the debtor's name as it appears on an unexpired driver's license issued by this State; and

(5) in situations where none of the above applies, if it uses:

(A) *only* the organizational name of the debtor if the debtor has a name; or

Example: Use the official name of a partnership.

(B) if the debtor has no name, *only* if it provides the names of each partner, member, associate and other person that comprise the debtor in a way that would be sufficient if the person was the debtor.

Example: If a partnership is so loosely organized that it doesn't use a name, then provide the names of each partner as described.

(b) A financing statement that provides the name of the debtor under (a) is not ineffective simply because it lacks:

(1) a trade name or other name of the debtor; or

(2) the names of each partner, member, associate or person that comprise the debtor, unless those names are required under (a)(5)(B).

End of Alternative B

(c) It's not sufficient if the financing statement only provides the trade name of the debtor.

Example: If an individual owns a sole proprietorship that operates the business under a name that differs from the individual's, it would not be sufficient to use *only* the business name. Instead, you should make sure the name of the individual owner is used on the financing statement.

(d) A financing statement is not insufficient just because it doesn't indicate that the secured party or a representative of the secured party are acting in a representative capacity for another person.

(e) You may put multiple debtors and secured parties onto one financing statement. Of course, this assumes that the parties all relate to a single relationship that the financing statement involves. This provision just means that there's no need to file a new financing statement for each additional debtor or secured party in the same transaction.

(f) For purposes of indicating the "name of the decedent" under (a)(2), use the decedent's name as shown on the order appointing the personal representative that was issued by the court having jurisdiction over the collateral.

Alternative B

(g) Use the most recently issued driver's license if there is more than one that fits the description in (a)(4)(C).

End of Alternative B

(h) "The "name of the settlor or testator" means:

(1) if the settlor or testator is a registered organization, the debtor's name as it currently appears on the public record of the jurisdiction where the debtor is organized; or

(2) in other cases, the name of the settlor or testator as shown in the document that formed the trust.

Why are there alternative forms of 9–503?

The alternatives given in 9–503 relate to individual debtors. The drafters of Article Nine thought that the debtor's name, as given on their driver's license, would be a useful point of reference for determining the proper name under which the secured party should file the financing statement. However, the drafters were aware that sometimes, states allow debtors to use characters or symbols on their driver's licenses that would not be accepted by the state's filing office, either due to the filing office's technological limitations or to the fact that the filing office's protocols for acceptable characters were not aligned with those of the state office issuing driver's licenses. Similarly, driver's licenses may allow for longer names than the filing office, or vice versa. If this happens, it might be impossible for the secured party to use the debtor's name as rendered on their driver's license for purposes of filing the financing statement. Thus, although the drafters wanted to encourage reference to the driver's license when possible (Alternative A), they created an alternative (Alternative B) for those states where the protocols for rendering names on driver's licenses might not be aligned with those for rendering names on a financing statement.

The Alternatives (A and B) are fairly recent additions to 9–503. It's possible that some jurisdictions may still use the 1999 form of 9–503, so we've included a plain English version of that below.

9–503 Original Form (1999)

(a) A financing statement sufficiently provides the debtor's name:

(1) if the debtor is a registered organization, then only if it provides the debtor's name as it appears on the public record **the registered organization filed in** ~~of~~ the jurisdiction where the debtor is organized;

(2) if the debtor is a descendant's estate, then only if it gives the name of the descendant and says we're dealing with an estate;

(3) if the debtor is a trust or a trustee, then only if it:

(A) provides the trust's name as listed in the document that formed the trust or if there's no specific name, then if it provides the name of the settler and enough information so you can tell which trust it is if the same settler is on other trusts; and

(B) indicates that the debtor is a trust or trustee acting on trust property; and

(4) In other cases:

(A) listing the debtor's individual organizational name (if it has one); and

(B) listing the names of the debtor's partners, members, or others comprising the debtor, if the debtor has no name.

(b) A financing statement that correctly provides the name of the debtor under (a) isn't ineffective just because it's missing:

(1) a trade name or other name of the debtor; or

(2) the names of partners, members, associates, or other persons who comprise the debtor unless (a)(4)(B) says they used to be listed.

(c) A financing statement is deficient if it supplies only the debtor's trade name.

(d) A financing statement is *not* deficient just because it doesn't indicate that the name listed for the secured party is really that party's representative, or if it doesn't list a representative of the secured party.

(e) You may put multiple debtors and secured parties onto one financing statement, assuming, of course, that the parties all relate to a single relationship the financing statement involves.

9–504: HOW TO DESCRIBE COLLATERAL IN A FINANCING STATEMENT

The description of collateral in a financing statement is good enough if (1) it describes the collateral in accordance with 9–108 or (2) it says something like it covers all assets or all personal property, even if that is not strictly true.

9–505: SPECIAL FINANCING STATEMENT RULES FOR CONSIGNMENTS, LEASES, BAILMENTS, AND CERTAIN OTHER TRANSACTIONS

(a) If a consignor, lessor or other bailor of goods, or a licensor or buyer of a payment intangible or promissory note prefers, they may either file a financing statement or comply with a statute or treaty under 9–311(a) using appropriately accurate terms other than "secured party" and "debtor" in those filings.

Example: This provision means it's okay if a lessor calls itself a "lessor" (rather than a "secured party") in a filing.

(b) When you're dealing with parties under (a) and there is a financing statement or some filing that is like a financing statement under 9–311(b), that filing does not automatically mean you're dealing with collateral securing an obligation. In other words, you may want to file a protective financing statement if there may be any doubt as to whether you're going to be considered a secured party. If you do make a protective filing, the filing can't be used as evidence to show you are a secured party if you prefer in the future to argue you are not one. If for a reason other than the filing it's determined later that you *are* a secured party, then your protective filing serves to perfect your security interest. . .it's a win-win for you, so you might as well do a protective filing.

9–506: WHAT ERRORS MAKE A FINANCING STATEMENT SERIOUSLY MISLEADING

(a) A financing statement is effective if it substantially satisfies Article Nine's requirements, even if it has errors or omissions, as long as those errors or omissions don't make the financing statement "seriously misleading."

(b) Except for (c), a financing statement is seriously misleading if it doesn't give the debtor's name in accordance with 9–503(a).

(c) If someone using the filing office's standard search logic to check its records under the debtor's correct name would turn up a financing statement that used an *incorrect* name of the debtor under 9–503(a), then the financing statement with the incorrect name is not seriously misleading.

(d) When you're dealing with 9–508(b), the "debtor's correct name" in subsection (c), above, means the correct name of the "new debtor."

9–507: EFFECTIVENESS OF A FINANCING STATEMENT IN LIGHT OF CHANGES

(a) A filed financing statement stays effective no matter what happens to the collateral and even if the collateral is sold or otherwise disposed of. This remains true even if the secured party knows about or consents to the disposition, so long as the secured party was not also consenting to the disposition without the security interest following the collateral.

Note: This provision represents the *general rule*, which is that the security interest and filed perfection follow the collateral unless the secured party specifically agrees that they don't, or unless some other rule (like 9–320's rule involving buyers in the ordinary course of business) cuts off enforcement of a security interest and therefore the effect of perfection.

(b) Except for (c) and 9–508, a filed financing statement stays effective even if the information in it later becomes seriously misleading. This means that a secured party need not amend the filing in order to take those changes into account—other than in the case of the exceptions, of course.

(c) If a debtor changes its name so that a filed financing statement becomes seriously misleading under 9–506:

(1) the financing statement still perfects a security interest in collateral acquired before the change and during the four months after the change; and

(2) the security interest stays effective to perfect a security interest in collateral acquired *after* four months from the name change only if the secured party *amends* the financing statement so it doesn't have a seriously misleading name anymore.

9–508: WHAT HAPPENS TO THE FINANCING STATEMENT WHEN A "NEW DEBTOR" COMES INTO THE PICTURE

(a) Except for all the exceptions in this section, a filed financing statement has the same effect of perfecting a security interest in collateral acquired by a "new debtor" as it had for the original debtor.

(b) If the difference in names between the original debtor and the "new debtor" makes a filed financing statement that is effective under (a) seriously misleading under 9–506:

(1) the financing statement still perfects a security interest in collateral acquired by the new debtor before and for four months after the new debtor becomes bound under 9–203(d); and

(2) the financing statement *doesn't* perfect a security interest in collateral acquired by the new debtor more than four months after the new debtor becomes bound under 9–203(d) unless a new *initial* financing statement with the name of the new debtor is filed before the end of the four month period.

Note: These rules apply when the new debtor is in the same jurisdiction as the original debtor. If there is a change of jurisdiction, use the rules in 9–316.

(c) This section doesn't apply if 9–507(a) makes a filed financing statement effective against the "new debtor."

9–509: WHO CAN FILE

(a) A person may file an initial financing statement or amendments that add collateral or debtors only if:

(1) the debtor authenticates a record that says it's okay to do that, or under (b) or (c); or

(2) the person holds an agricultural lien that became effective at the time of filing and the financing statement covers *only* collateral in which the person holds an agricultural lien. In this situation, the debtor's consent isn't needed because the lien arises as a matter of non-Article Nine law.

(b) When the debtor authenticates or becomes bound as a debtor by a security agreement, the debtor or new debtor authorizes filing of an initial financing statement and any amendment that covers:

(1) the collateral described in the security agreement; and

(2) property that becomes covered as proceeds under 9–315(a)(2), even if the security agreement didn't expressly cover proceeds.

(c) By acquiring collateral covered by a security interest or agricultural lien under 9–315(a)(1), a debtor is authorizing the filing of an initial financing statement and an amendment covering the collateral and property that becomes covered as proceeds under 9–315(a)(2).

Note: This provision means that because someone who obtains property that was collateral when in the hands of their transferor becomes a debtor to the secured party in that collateral, the secured party (1) has the right to file an initial financing statement naming the transferee as its debtor and also (2) has the right to amend the prior financing statement with its original debtor so that statement now covers the proceeds received as a result of the transfer.

(d) A person may file an amendment other than an amendment adding collateral or a debtor to a financing statement only if:

(1) the secured party of record authorizes it; or

(2) the amendment is a termination statement that the secured party hasn't filed as required under 9–513(a) or (c), the debtor says it's okay to file the termination statement, and the termination statement indicates the debtor's authorization.

(e) If there is more than one secured party of record for a financing statement, each one may on its own authorize an amendment filing under (d).

9–510: AUTHORIZATION AND EFFECTIVENESS OF FINANCING STATEMENTS

(a) For a filing to be effective, it has to be filed by someone authorized under 9–509.

(b) A record that one secured party authorizes to be filed doesn't affect the rights and powers of another secured party on that same financing statement.

(c) A continuation statement isn't effective unless it's filed within the six-month period set by 9–515(d).

9–511: THE SECURED PARTY OF RECORD

(a) A "secured party of record" is whoever's name is listed on a financing statement as a secured party or a representative of the secured party in an initial financing statement. If an initial financing statement is filed under 9–514(a), the assignee listed there is the secured party of record.

(b) A person who's named as a secured party or a representative of a secured party in an amendment to a financing statement is a secured party of record. If an amendment is filed under 9–514(b) regarding assignments of a secured party's rights, the assignee listed there is the secured party of record.

(c) A person stays a secured party of record until an amendment is filed that deletes that person from the record.

9–512 ALT A: AMENDING A FINANCING STATEMENT

Alternative A

(a) Except for 9–509, a secured party can add or delete collateral or continue or terminate or, subject to (e), amend a financing statement by filing an amendment that:

(1) uses the file number to identify the initial financing statement being amended; and

(2) provides the information required in 9–502(b) if the amendment is for an initial financing statement filed or recorded in a real estate filing office described in 9–501(a)(1) (regarding fixture filings).

End of Alternative A

(b) Except for 9–515, filing an amendment doesn't extend the length of time a financing statement is effective.

(c) An amendment that adds collateral is effective for that collateral only from the date the amendment is filed.

(d) An amendment that adds a debtor is effective for that debtor only from the date that amendment is filed.

(e) An amendment is ineffective if it:

(1) deletes all debtors but doesn't supply a debtor's name as a replacement; or

(2) deletes all secured parties of record but doesn't supply a secured party's name as a replacement.

9–512 ALT B: AMENDING A FINANCING STATEMENT

Alternative B

(a) Except for 9–509, a secured party can add or delete collateral or continue or terminate or, subject to (e), amend a financing statement by filing an amendment that:

(1) uses the file number to identify the initial financing statement being amended; and

(2) provides the information required in 9–502(b) if the amendment is for an initial financing statement filed or recorded in a real estate filing office described in 9–501(a)(1) (regarding fixture filings), and also provides the date [and time] when the initial financing statement was filed.

End of Alternative B

(b) Except for 9–515, filing an amendment doesn't extend the length of time a financing statement is effective.

(c) An amendment that adds collateral is effective for that collateral only from the date the amendment is filed.

(d) An amendment that adds a debtor is effective for that debtor only from the date the amendment is filed.

(e) An amendment is ineffective if it:

(1) deletes all debtors but doesn't supply a debtor's name as a replacement; or

(2) deletes all secured parties of record but doesn't supply a secured party's name as a replacement.

Why are there alternative forms of 9–512?

The drafters recognized that real estate filing offices in some states require more information in amendments. In addition, some real estate filing offices can't search their records by both the debtor's name and the filing number. The drafters provided Alternative B to 9–512(a) for those states.

9–513: FILING A TERMINATION STATEMENT

(a) A secured party must make a secured party of record terminate a financing statement that covers consumer goods and:

(1) there is no obligation left to be secured by the collateral and no commitment to give other value; or

(2) the debtor didn't authorize the filing of the initial financing statement.

(b) To comply with (a), the termination statement must be filed:

(1) within a month after the secured obligation is eliminated and there is no commitment give any more value; or

(2) if earlier than within one month, then within 20 days after the secured party receives an authenticated demand from a debtor.

(c) In *non-consumer* situations and consumer situations that don't fit in (a), within 20 days after a secured party receives an authenticated demand from a debtor, the secured party must make the secured party of record send the debtor a termination statement or file the termination statement itself if:

(1) there is no obligation left to be secured by the collateral and no commitment to give value, except for situations involving sales of accounts or chattel paper or goods under consignment;

(2) the financing statement covers the sale of accounts or chattel paper but the person obligated to pay has discharged its obligation;

(3) the financing statement covers consigned goods that are not in the debtor's possession; or

(4) the debtor didn't authorize the filing of the initial financing statement.

(d) Except for 9–510, as soon as a termination statement is filed, it cancels the financing statement it applies to. Except for 9–510, when you're dealing with 9–519(g) (removing a debtor's name), 9–522(a) (maintaining records of a filing after lapse), and 9–523(c) (filing office providing information), a termination statement filing indicating that it relates to a debtor that is a transmitting utility also cancels the financing statement it applies to.

9–514: WHEN THE SECURED PARTY ASSIGNS ITS POWER TO AUTHORIZE AMENDMENTS

(a) Except for (c), an initial financing statement may show the secured party has assigned its power to authorize amendments by providing the name and address of the assignee as if they were the name and address of the secured party.

(b) Except for (c), a secured party may assign for the record all or part of its power to authorize amendments by filing an amendment that:

(1) uses the file number to identify the initial financing statement;

(2) provides the assignor's name; and

(3) provides the assignee's name and mailing address.

(c) If a mortgage serves as a fixture filing under 9–502(c), use the real estate recording rules to record an assignment of a security interest in the fixture.

9–515: WHEN A FINANCING STATEMENT LAPSES, AND HOW TO FILE A CONTINUATION STATEMENT

(a) Except for (b), (e), (f), and (g), a financing statement is good for five years from the date of filing.

(b) Except for (e), (f), and (g), an initial financing statement for a public finance or manufactured-home transaction is good for 30 years, so long as the filing indicates it's for one of those types of transactions.

(c) Unless a continuation statement is filed in accordance with (d), a filed financing statement lapses at the end of its effective period. Once it lapses, a filed financing statement is ineffective and any security interest or agricultural lien it perfected becomes unperfected unless there is continuous perfection in some other way. Once the security interest or agricultural lien becomes unperfected, it's as if it was never perfected against another security interest or other purchaser for value.

Note: See 1–201(b)(29) & (30) for the definitions of "purchase" and "purchaser."

(d) A continuation statement may be filed *only* in the six months *before* the five year period in (a) expires. If (b) applies, a continuation statement may be filed *only* in the six months *before* the 30-year period expires.

(e) Except for 9–510, if a continuation statement is timely filed, the initial financing stays effective for another five years from the day on which it would have become ineffective without the continuation filing. At the end of that next five-year period, the financing statement lapses as it would under (c), unless another continuation statement is filed under (d). If you want, you can keep the original filing in force forever by filing a continuation statement under (d) as the end of each five-year period approaches.

(f) If a transmitting utility is involved, and the financing statement says so, the financing statement is effective until a termination statement is filed.

(g) If a recorded mortgage is serving as a fixture filing under 9–502(c), it is effective until the mortgage is released or satisfied or its effectiveness otherwise ends as to the real estate.

9–516: WHEN "FILING" OCCURS (AND DOESN'T)

(a) Except for (b), "filing" occurs when a record has been communicated to a filing office and the filing fee is tendered, or when the office accepts the record.

(b) There is no "filing" if the filing office refuses to accept a record because:

(1) the record isn't communicated in a way that office authorizes;

(2) the filing fee isn't tendered;

Note: If someone tenders *more* than the filing fee, the filing office will treat it as if the correct fee was tendered.

(3) the office can't index the record because:

(A) the record is an initial financing statement that lacks the debtor's name;

(B) the record is an amendment or correction statement that: (i) doesn't identify the initial financing statement as required by 8–512 or 9–518; or (ii) identifies a financing statement that lapsed under 9–515;

(C) either (i) the record doesn't identify an individual debtor's last name and is an initial financing statement; or (ii) the record is an amendment that uses a name of the debtor that wasn't used in the initial financing statement; or

(D) the record doesn't have a sufficient description of the real estate involved if it's a fixture filing or recording under 9–501(a)(1).

(4) the name and mailing address of the secured party of record isn't included, if you're dealing with an initial financing statement or an amendment adding a secured party;

(5) The record is an initial financing statement or an amendment providing the name of a debtor that wasn't included in the initial financing statement and it fails to:

(A) provide the debtor's mailing address;

(B) indicate whether the debtor is an individual or an organization; or

(C) in the case of a debtor who's an organization provide (i) the type of organization; (ii) the debtor's jurisdiction of organization; or (iii) an organization identification number for the debtor (or to state there isn't one);

(6) the record doesn't give the name and mailing address of the assignee if you're dealing with an initial financing statement under 9–514(a) or an amendment under 9–514(b); or

(7) the record is a continuation statement that isn't filed within the six-month period designated in 9–515(d).

(c) For purposes of (b),

(1) a record doesn't provide information if that information is illegible or indecipherable; and

(2) treat the filing as an initial financing statement if the record doesn't indicate it's an amendment or doesn't identify the initial financing statement it relates to as required by 9–512, 9–514, or 9–518.

(d) If a record is communicated to a filing office with tender of the filing fee, but the office refuses to accept it for a reason not included in (b), then the record is still effective against everyone except a purchaser for value, including another secured party, who gave value in reasonable reliance on the fact there was no record in the files.

9–517: WHEN THE FILING OFFICE MAKES A MISTAKE

A filed record is effective even if the filing office screws up the indexing of the record. In other words, if the filing office files under the wrong name, as long as the filing otherwise meets the requirements for a correct filing, the secured party is protected as if the name had been entered in the right place. This means later searchers, rather than the original filer, bear the risk of an incorrect indexing.

9–518 ALT A: FILING AN INFORMATION STATEMENT

(a) A person who thinks a record under their name is inadequate or was wrongfully filed may file an information statement that says how they think the record should read or why it shouldn't have been filed.

Note: An information statement doesn't invalidate the record; it just explains the problem the person filing the statement has with the record. See (e).

Alternative A

(b) An information statement under (a) must:

(1) identify the file number assigned to the initial financing statement the statement relates to;

(2) indicate it's an information statement; and

(3) give the reason the person believes the record:

(A) was wrongfully filed, or

(B) isn't accurate and explain how the inaccuracy should be cured through amendment.

End of Alternative A

(c) A secured party of record regarding the financing statement on which the information statement was filed may file their own information statement explaining why they think the complaining party wasn't entitled to file their statement under the terms of 9–509(d).

Alternative A

(d) An information statement under (c) must:

(1) identify the file number assigned to the initial financing statement the statement relates to;

(2) indicate it's an information statement; and

(3) give the reason the person believes the person who filed the information statement wasn't entitled to do so under the terms of 9–509(d).

End of Alternative A

(e) A record, including an initial financing statement, is still effective even if a correction statement is filed.

9–518 ALT B: FILING AN INFORMATION STATEMENT

(a) A person who thinks a record under their name is inadequate or was wrongfully filed may file an information statement that says how they think the record should read or why it shouldn't have been filed.

Note: An information statement doesn't invalidate the record; it just explains the problem the person filing the statement has with the record. See (e).

Alternative B

(b) An information statement under (a) must:

(1) identify the record to which it relates by:

(A) identifying the file number assigned to the initial financing statement the statement relates to; and

(B) if the record was filed as a fixture filing, state the date [and time] the initial financing statement was filed [or recorded] and the information that 9–502(b) specifies;

(2) indicate it's an information statement; and

(3) give the reason the person believes the record:

(A) was wrongfully filed, or

(B) isn't accurate and explain how the inaccuracy should be cured through amendment.

End of Alternative B

(c) A secured party of record regarding the financing statement on which the information statement was filed may file their own information statement explaining why they think the complaining party wasn't entitled to file their statement under the terms of 9–509(d).

Alternative B

(d) An information statement under (c) must:

(1) identify:

(A) the file number assigned to the initial financing statement the statement relates to; and

(B) if the record was filed as a fixture filing, state the date [and time] the initial financing statement was filed [or recorded] and the information that 9–502(b) specifies;

(2) indicate it's an information statement; and

(3) give the reason the person believes the person who filed the information statement wasn't entitled to do so under the terms of 9–509(d).

End of Alternative B

(e) A record, including an initial financing statement, is still effective even if a correction statement is filed.

Why are there alternative forms of 9–518?

The drafters recognized that real estate filing offices in some states require more information in amendments. In addition, some real estate filing offices can't search their records by both the debtor's name and the filing number. The drafters provided Alternative B to 9–518(b) and (d) for those states.

9–519 ALT A: HOW TO INDEX AND COMMUNICATE INFORMATION ON RECORDS

(a) For each record filed, the filing office must:

(1) assign a unique number to the record;

(2) create its own record of the number, filing date and time of the filed record;

(3) keep the filed record for public inspection; and

(4) index the filed record following the requirements of (c), (d), and (e).

(b) A file number must include a digit that:

(1) fits a mathematical scheme related to the other digits in the file number; and

(2) helps the filing office figure out whether a number someone uses in a later filing includes a single-digit or transpositional error.

(c) Except for (d) and (e), the filing office must:

(1) index the initial financing statement under the debtor's name and index with that statement any later filings related to the statement; and

(2) index a record that has a new name for a debtor under both the new name and the old name.

(d) If a financing statement is a fixture filing or covers as-extracted collateral or timber to be cut, it must be indexed:

(1) under the debtor's name and each owner of record's name as if they were mortgagors of the real estate; and

(2) if the State provides for indexing under the mortgagee's name, then index that way using the secured party's name as mortgagee, or if real estate indexing is by description of the property, then do it that way as if the financing statement was a recording of a mortgage on the real estate.

(e) If a financing statement is a fixture filing or covers as-extracted collateral or timber to be cut, the filing office must index an assignment under 9–514(a) or an amendment under 9–514(b):

(1) under the name of the assignor as grantor; and

(2) under the assignee's name to the extent this state's law provides for indexing that way for an assignee of a mortgage.

Alternative A

(f) The filing office must maintain a capability:

(1) to retrieve a record by the debtor's name and the filing number of the initial financing statement; and

(2) to associate and retrieve together all the records that relate to an initial financing statement.

End of Alternative A

(g) The filing office must keep the debtor's name in the index for at least one year after a financing statement lapses due to time under 9–515 as to *all* secured parties of record.

(h) The filing office may create rules for when and how it needs to fulfill the requirements of (a) through (e), but it has to fulfill those requirements no later than two business days after the filing office receives the record that is to be filed.

9–519 ALT B: HOW TO INDEX AND COMMUNICATE INFORMATION ON RECORDS

(a) For each record filed, the filing office must:

(1) assign a unique number to the record;

(2) create its own record of the number, filing date and time of the filed record;

(3) keep the filed record for public inspection; and

(4) index the filed record following the requirements of (c), (d), and (e).

(b) A file number must include a digit that:

(1) fits a mathematical scheme related to the other digits in the file number; and

(2) helps the filing office figure out whether a number someone uses in a later filing includes a single-digit or transpositional error.

(c) Except for (d) and (e), the filing office must:

(1) index the initial financing statement under the debtor's name and index with that statement any later filings related to the statement; and

(2) index a record that has a new name for a debtor under both the new name and the old name.

(d) If a financing statement is a fixture filing or covers as-extracted collateral or timber to be cut, it must be indexed:

(1) under the debtor's name and each owner of record's name as if they were mortgagors of the real estate; and

(2) if the State provides for indexing under the mortgagee's name, then index that way using the secured party's name as mortgagee, or if real estate indexing is by description of the property, then do it that way as if the financing statement was a recording of a mortgage on the real estate.

(e) If a financing statement is a fixture filing or covers as-extracted collateral or timber to be cut, the filing office must index an assignment under 9–514(a) or an amendment under 9–514(b):

(1) under the name of the assignor as grantor; and

(2) under the name of the assignee to the extent this state's law provides for indexing that way for an assignee of a mortgage.

Alternative B

(f) The filing office must maintain a capability:

(1) to retrieve a record by the debtor's name and:

(A) for a filing office described in 9–501(a)(1), by the number of the initial financing statement and the date [and time] that the record was filed [or recorded]; and

(B) for a filing office described in 9–501(a)(2), by the number of the initial financing statement; and

(2) to associate and retrieve together all the records that relate to an initial financing statement.

End of Alternative B

(g) The filing office must keep the debtor's name in the index for at least one year after a financing statement lapses due to time under 9–515 as to *all* secured parties of record.

(h) The filing office may create rules for when and how it needs to fulfill the requirements of (a) through (e), but it has to fulfill those requirements no later than two business days after the filing office receives the record that is to be filed.

Why are there alternative forms of 9–519?

The drafters recognized that real estate filing offices in some states require more information in amendments. In addition, some real estate filing offices can't search their records by both the debtor's name and the filing number. The drafters provided Alternative B to 9–519(f) for those states.

9–520: FILING OFFICE'S REFUSAL TO FILE A RECORD

(a) A filing office *must* refuse to file a record if it violates 9–516(b)'s rules, but those rules are the only ones it may use as a basis not to file the record.

(b) The filing office must let the filing party know if it refuses to file a record, and it has to explain the reason for non-filing and give the date and time the record would have been filed if it hadn't been refused. This notice must be made within two days after receipt of the record and may be made in accordance with the office's individual rules.

(c) A financing statement that satisfies 9–502(a) and (b) is effective if the filing office files it even if the filing office is supposed to refuse to file it because of (a), above. But 9–338 applies if the financing statement provides information of the type found in 9–516(b)(5) that is incorrect at the time of filing.

(d) If a record relates to multiple debtors, the rules in this section apply to each debtor separately. This means that a record may be partially effective for filing.

9–521: FORM OF FINANCING STATEMENT

(a) A filing office must accept a financing statement if it's on a form like that in 9–521, unless there's a 9–516(b) reason not to accept it.

(b) Ditto for amendments.

9–522 ALT A: KEEPING AND DESTROYING FINANCING STATEMENTS

Alternative A

(a) The filing office must keep the information in a filed financing statement for at least one year after a financing statement lapses under 9–515 as to *all* secured parties. This information must be retrievable by using the debtor's name or the file number assigned to the initial financing statement.

End of Alternative A

(b) A filing office may destroy the written record of a financing statement if its destruction doesn't violate another statute, so long as it keeps a record of the financing statement that complies with (a).

9–522 ALT B: KEEPING AND DESTROYING FINANCING STATEMENTS

Alternative B

(a) The filing office must keep the information in a filed financing statement for at least one year after a financing statement lapses under 9–515 as to *all* secured parties. This information must be retrievable by using the debtor's name and:

(1) for a filing office described in 9–501(a)(1), by the number of the initial financing statement and the date [and time] that the record was filed [or recorded]; or

(2) for a filing office described in 9–501(a)(2), by the number of the initial financing statement.

End of Alternative B

(b) A filing office may destroy the written record of a financing statement if its destruction doesn't violate another statute, so long as it keeps a record of the financing statement that complies with (a).

Why are there alternative forms of 9–522?

The drafters recognized that real estate filing offices in some states require more information in amendments. In addition, some real estate filing offices can't search their records by both the debtor's name and the filing number. The drafters provided Alternative B to 9–522(a) for those states.

9–523: INFORMATION FROM THE FILING OFFICE

(a) If someone filing a record asks for one, the filing office must send a copy that shows the number assigned under 9–519(a)(1) and the date and time the record was filed. If the filer provides an extra copy of the record, the filing office instead may put the 9–519(a)(1) number and filing date and time on the copy and send it back to the filer.

(b) If the filed record is not in writing (e.g., an electronic filing), the filing office must provide the person who filed it an acknowledgement that provides the information in the record, the 9–519(a)(1) number and the filing date and time.

(c) The filing office must provide or make available a record of the following information to anyone who asks for it:

(1) Whether there is or was on file up to three business days before the filing office receives the request (***Note***: the office may designate the time and date from which it's counting back), a financing statement that:

(A) designates a particular debtor, or, if requested, a debtor at an address specified by the requestor;

(B) has not lapsed under 9–515 with respect to all secured parties of record; and

(C) if the request specifies, has lapsed under 9–515 but which still has records maintained under 9–522(a)

(2) The date and time each financing statement was filed; and

(3) The information provided in each financing statement.

(d) A filing office may use any medium to provide the information under (c). Upon request, the filing office must provide information by issuing [a written certificate] [or a record that is self-authenticating for in-court purposes].

(e) The filing office may make its own rules for fulfilling its obligations under (a) through (d), so long as it provides the information within two business days after receiving the request.

(f) At least once a week [the filing office or someone else who is designated] must make available to the public in bulk copies of all records filed with the office in every medium the filing office uses to accept filings.

9–524: WHEN FILING OFFICE IS EXCUSED

The filing office is excused from the time limits to fulfill its obligations under the 9–500s if it can't do so because its computers or other equipment fail or otherwise glitch, or if there are things that happen beyond its control, so long as the office is reasonably diligent under the circumstances.

9–525: FILING FEES

(a) The filing office may vary what it charges a filer depending on the length or type of medium used to convey the filing. Here are the charges:___________

(b) [Ditto for public-finance and manufactured-housing transactions]

(c) [**Alternative A**: The filing office may not charge more based on the number of names that need to be indexed in a filing.] [**Alternative B** allows variable charges based on the number of names to be included.]

(d) The filing office may vary the charge for responding to a request for information based on what medium is used to make the request. Here are the charges:_______

(e) If a mortgage is also going to serve as a fixture filing or to cover as-extracted collateral or timber to be cut under 9–502(c), the filing office may not charge a fee separate from the recording and satisfaction fees that apply to a mortgage filing.

Note: The drafters have encouraged states to adopt Alternative A for 9–525(c) unless it is substantially more expensive for the state to index additional names.

9–526: FILING OFFICE RULES

(a) The [proper government authority] must adopt and publish rules to implement Article Nine. The filing office rules must be consistent with Article Nine and adopted in accordance with [whatever regular administrative rule adoption laws specify].

(b) [The legislature should designate an agency] to consult with other jurisdictions using the Revised Article Nine, to keep up with the Model Rules suggested by the International Association of Corporate Administration, and to keep up with the rules and technologies used by other jurisdictions when they implement Article Nine. This is to help all jurisdictions communicate with each other more easily and to promote consistency for searchers from any jurisdiction, thus bringing harmony to the world.

9–527: REPORT ON THE FILING OFFICE'S OPERATIONS

[The appropriate government authority] shall report [annually or on a specific date] on how the filing office is operating. The report must state the extent:

(1) to which the office's rules are not in harmony with those of other jurisdictions that adopted Revised Article Nine; and

(2) to which the office's rules are not in harmony with the most recent version of the Model Rules specified in 9–526, and explain the reasons for any differences.

INTRODUCTION TO THE 9–600s

The 9–600s ("Part 6" of Article Nine) are the provisions of Article Nine governing default on and enforcement of security interests. Here you'll find information about what happens after default, the rules secured parties (and others with interests in collateral) must follow when it comes to asserting their rights upon default, and the rights and remedies available if the secured party does not comply with the rules listed.

9–601: RIGHTS AFTER DEFAULT

(a) After default, the secured party has the rights provided in the 9–600s (such as self-help repossession), and, except for the 9–602 rules, any other rights the parties agreed to. Along with any rights and procedures under the 9–600s, a secured party may also:

(1) go outside Article Nine to get a court judgment or foreclose or enforce its claim by any judicial procedure; and

(2) proceed against documents or the goods they cover if the collateral is the documents.

(b) A secured party in possession or control of collateral under 7–106, 9–104, 9–105, 9–106, or 9–107 has the rights and duties in 9–207.

(c) The rights under (a) and (b) exist together, and the secured party may exercise them at the same time. In other words, the secured party doesn't have to choose an exclusive remedy.

(d) Except for (g) and 9–605, after default a debtor and an obligor have the rights provided in the 9–600s and any other rights the parties agreed to.

(e) If a secured party reduces its claim to judgment, the lien that is created for any levy that may be made on the collateral when executing on the judgment relates back to the *earliest* of:

(1) the date the security interest or agricultural lien was perfected;

(2) the date a financing statement was filed to cover the collateral; or

(3) the date specified by an agricultural lien statute.

(f) A sale of collateral that takes place after execution is considered a "foreclosure by judicial procedure." A secured party may purchase collateral at the sale and thereby take it free of any other requirements of Article Nine.

(g) Except for 9–607(c), the 9–600s add no duties to a secured party that is a consignor or a buyer of accounts, chattel paper, payment intangibles, or promissory notes.

9–602: RULES THAT CANNOT BE WAIVED OR VARIED

Except for 9–624, the debtor or obligor may not waive or vary the rules in the sections listed in the regular body of 9–602.

Note: Please read 9–602 if you want to know which rules can't be waived or varied. There's no point in us reproducing the list here.

9–603: PARTIES' AGREEMENT ON STANDARDS

(a) The parties may agree to standards that determine whether their respective rights and duties have been met under a rule listed in 9–602 if the standards are not manifestly unreasonable.

(b) The rule in (a) doesn't apply to the 9–609 duty to refrain from breaching the peace.

9–604: THE SECURED PARTY'S OPTIONS IF THE SECURITY AGREEMENT COVERS REAL PROPERTY OR FIXTURES

(a) If a security agreement covers both personal property and real estate, a secured party may proceed:

(1) under Article Nine against the personal property but separately use its rights regarding the real estate; or

(2) against both the personal property and real estate using real estate law, but that means it's giving up its Article Nine remedies.

(b) Except for (c), if a security agreement covers fixtures, a secured party may proceed:

(1) using the 9–600s; or

(2) using real estate law, but that means it's giving up its Article Nine remedies.

(c) Except for contrary parts of Article Nine, if a secured party has a priority right to fixtures over the owner and encumbrancers of the real estate, the secured party may remove the fixtures if there's a default.

(d) A secured party that removes collateral must promptly reimburse an encumbrancer or owner of the real estate (if they're not also the debtor) for the cost to repair any physical damage to the property due to removal. However, the secured party is not responsible for any reduction in value of the property due to removal or for the necessity of replacing whatever was removed. A party entitled to reimbursement may refuse permission to remove fixtures until the secured party assures them that reimbursement will occur.

Note: An escrow or similar idea would work for assuring reimbursement.

9–605: LIMITATION OF SECURED PARTY'S DUTIES

A secured party has no duty:

(1) to a debtor or obligor unless the secured party knows that's what they are, knows their identity and knows how to communicate with them; or

(2) to another secured party or a lien holder that filed a financing statement against a person unless the secured party knows the person is a debtor and knows the person's identity.

9–606: WHEN A DEFAULT OCCURS ON AN AGRICULTURAL LIEN

For purposes of the 9–600s, a default on an agricultural lien occurs when the secured party becomes entitled to enforce the lien under the terms of the statute that created it.

9–607: SECURED PARTY'S OPTIONS FOR COLLECTION AND ENFORCEMENT OF RIGHTS

(a) When dealing with rights to payment (like accounts) that have been used as collateral, if the parties have agreed, or if there is a default, a secured party may:

(1) tell an account debtor or someone else obligated on the collateral to pay the secured party or otherwise perform on the obligation;

(2) take any proceeds they're entitled to under 9–315;

(3) enforce the rights the secured party's debtor had against the account debtor or other obligated party to get payment or otherwise perform on the obligation, including going against any property that served as collateral for the obligation;

(4) apply the balance of a deposit account to an obligation secured by the deposit account, if the secured party is a bank that perfected by control under 9–104(a)(1); and

(5) instruct the bank to pay the deposit account to or for the benefit of the secured party if the secured party perfected by control under 9–104(a)(2) or (3).

(b) If it's necessary for a secured party to exercise (under (a)(3)) the debtor's right to enforce a mortgage without having to go to court, the secured party may record in the office where a record of the mortgage is recorded:

(1) a copy of the security agreement that shows a security interest in the obligation the mortgage secures; and

(2) the secured party's sworn affidavit in recordable form stating that a default has occurred and the secured party is entitled to enforce the mortgage without going to court.

(c) A secured party must act in a commercially reasonable manner:

(1) to collect or enforce an account debtor's or other person's obligation on the collateral; and

(2) if it is entitled to charge back in whole or in part to the debtor the value of any collateral it can't collect on (such as an uncollectible account).

Note: Subsection (c) says that if the secured party is enforcing the debt the account debtor had owed to the secured party's debtor, the secured party has to do two things. First, it has to be reasonable in how it deals with the account debtor. Second, it has to get as much of the debt paid *by the account debtor* as it reasonably can if it's allowed to go after the original debtor for any amount it can't collect from the account debtor. This is because it wouldn't be fair to the debtor to go unreasonably easy on the account debtor on the assumption that the secured party can just squeeze money out of the original debtor for whatever isn't paid.

(d) A secured party may deduct its reasonable collection and enforcement expenses, including legal fees and expenses, from what it collects under (c).

(e) This section doesn't control whether an account debtor, bank or other person obligated on collateral owes a duty to a secured party. If any duty is owed, that will be controlled by other law.

9–608: APPLICATION OF PROCEEDS GENERATED FROM COLLECTION OR ENFORCEMENT

(a) If a security interest or agricultural lien secures payment or performance of an obligation, use these rules to determine how the proceeds generated from collection on the obligation should be applied:

(1) If you're dealing with cash proceeds generated by collecting or enforcing payment under 9–607, apply the cash proceeds in the following order:

(A) the secured party's reasonable expenses of collecting and enforcing, including whatever the parties have agreed to for legal fees and expenses that is within the law;

(B) satisfying the obligations that were secured; and

(C) satisfying obligations due a subordinate security interest in the collateral, so long as the foreclosing secured party receives an authenticated demand from the subordinate party before the proceeds have been completely distributed.

(2) A subordinate interest must provide reasonable proof of its interest or lien within a reasonable time after being asked by the higher-priority security interest holder. Unless they comply with the request, the priority interest does not need to honor a demand under (1)(c).

(3) A secured party does not have to apply or pay over noncash proceeds under 9–607 unless it would be commercially unreasonable not to, and the secured party must apply the noncash proceeds in a commercially reasonable manner when it does apply them.

Example: If an account debtor executes a promissory note to the foreclosing secured party, the secured party doesn't need to apply right away the whole amount due under the note to reduce the amount its own debtor owes to it. Instead, the secured party may apply receipts from the promissory note as it collects them over time.

(4) A secured party must let its debtor know if it has any surplus from its collections, and pay that surplus to the debtor. Unless the parties agree otherwise, an obligor is responsible for any deficiency.

(b) If you're dealing with a *sale* of accounts, chattel papers, payment intangibles, or promissory notes, the debtor is not entitled to any surplus and the obligor is not liable for a deficiency, unless the parties agree otherwise.

9–609: POST-DEFAULT REPOSSESSION RIGHTS

(a) After default, a secured party:

(1) may take possession of the collateral; and

(2) may leave equipment with the debtor but disable it and then dispose of it by sale or otherwise at the debtor's location under 9–610.

(b) A secured party may repossess under (a):

(1) using the courts; or

(2) without using the courts so long as there is no breach of the peace.

Note: Repossessing without using the courts is also referred to as "self-help repossession."

(c) If the parties agree ahead of time, and if not then automatically after default, a secured party may require the debtor to collect the collateral and bring it to a place that is reasonably convenient for both parties.

9–610: DISPOSITION OF COLLATERAL

(a) Once a default occurs, a secured party may dispose of some or all of the collateral in any way, in whatever condition it's in, or after any commercially reasonable preparation or processing.

(b) Every aspect of a disposition of collateral must be commercially reasonable. This includes method, time, place, and so on. So long as it's commercially reasonable, a secured party may dispose of the collateral by public or private sale, and may sell it off in parts and whenever and wherever it chooses on whatever terms it likes.

(c) A secured party may purchase the collateral that was the subject of the security agreement:

(1) at a public sale; or

(2) at a private sale *only* if that type of collateral has a regular, recognized market or it's the subject of widely distributed standard price quotations—for example, stocks traded on an exchange.

(d) The standard warranties relating to good title, possession, etc., that would accompany any sale apply when a secured party sells off the collateral.

(e) A secured party may disclaim or modify warranties under (d):

(1) in whatever ways would be allowable in any sale; or

(2) by communicating to the purchaser a record that shows a contract for sale to the purchaser that expressly disclaims or modifies the warranties.

(f) A record is sufficient under (e) if it says something indicating there is no warranty of title, possession, etc., in the sale.

9–611: NOTIFICATION OF DISPOSITION

(a) In this section, "notification date" means the earlier of the date on which:

(1) a secured party sends to the debtor or any secondary obligor, like a guarantor, an authenticated notice of disposition; or

(2) the debtor and any secondary obligor waive their right to notification.

(b) Except for (d), a secured party that disposes of collateral under 9–610 must send a reasonable, authenticated notice of disposition to people specified in (c).

(c) To comply with (b), a secured party must send an authenticated notification of disposition to:

(1) the debtor;

(2) any secondary obligor; and

(3) if the collateral is *not* consumer goods:

(A) any other person who, before the notification date, has sent the secured party an authenticated notice that the person claims an interest in the collateral;

(B) any other secured party or lien holder who, at least 10 days before the notification date, held a security interest or lien perfected by a filed financing statement that:

(i) identifies the collateral;

(ii) is indexed under the debtor's name as of that date; and

(iii) is filed in the correct office for such filings as of that date;

and

(C) any other secured party that, at least 10 days before the notification date, held a security interest perfected by complying with a statute, regulation or treaty under 9–311(a).

(d) Don't apply (b) if the collateral is perishable, will quickly lose value, or is a type customarily sold on a recognized market.

(e) A secured party complies with (c)(3)(B)'s notification requirement if:

(1) between 20 and 30 days before the notification date the secured party reasonably requests information on financing statements indexed under the debtor's name in the office indicated in (c)(3)(B); and

(2) before the notification date, the secured party:

(A) did not receive a response to the request; or

(B) received a response to the request and sent an authenticated notice of disposition to everyone named in the response who had a financing statement that covered the collateral.

9–612: WHEN A NOTIFICATION IS SENT WITHIN A REASONABLE TIME

(a) Except for (b), it's a question of fact whether a notification is sent within a reasonable time.

(b) In a *non-consumer* transaction, a notification of disposition is sent in a reasonable time if it is sent after default and at least 10 days before the time the notice specifies for disposition.

9–613: CONTENTS OF THE NOTIFICATION

In *non-consumer*-goods transactions, use these rules:

(1) The contents of a notification of disposition are good enough if they:

(A) describe the debtor and secured party;

(B) describe the collateral that is going to be disposed of;

(C) state how the disposition will be made;

(D) state that the debtor may have an accounting of the unpaid indebtedness, and say how much the accounting will cost; and

(E) state when and where a public disposition will be made.

(2) It's a question of fact whether a notice is still sufficient even if it lacks information in (1).

(3) If a notice supplies substantially the information in (1), it's good even if it includes:

(A) information not specified in (1); or

(B) minor errors that are not seriously misleading.

(4) There is no requirement that the notification use any specific phrasing.

(5) You've provided sufficient information if you use completed forms like those in the Official Version of 9–613 regarding notification of disposition and in paragraph 9–614(3) regarding notice of the plan to sell the collateral.

Note: Please check those forms out for yourself in the Official Version.

9–614: CONTENTS OF THE NOTIFICATION FOR CONSUMER-GOODS TRANSACTIONS

In consumer-goods transactions, use these rules:

(1) A notification of disposition must have:

(A) the 9–613(1) information;

(B) a description of any amounts owed for deficiency by the person who the notice is sent to;

(C) a telephone number that may be called to find out the amount it will cost to redeem the collateral under 9–623; and

(D) a telephone number or mailing address to be used to get additional information on the disposition and the obligation that was secured.

(2) There is no requirement that the notification use any specific phrasing.

(3) [Check out the form in 9–614(3) of the Official Version for the sanctioned version of the notice of how the collateral will be sold.]

(4) If you use the form in (3), that's sufficient even if you add more information at the end of the form.

(5) If you use the form in (3), that's sufficient even if you add verbiage that (1) doesn't require, and that verbiage is wrong. However, it's not sufficient if the wrong verbiage you added could mislead someone regarding their Article Nine rights.

(6) If you don't use the form in (3) for your notice, then use law outside of Article Nine to determine the effect of including information that (1) doesn't require.

9–615: HOW TO APPLY PROCEEDS GENERATED BY A DISPOSITION

(a) A secured party must apply or pay over (so they can be applied) the cash proceeds generated by a disposition under **9–610** in the following order to:

(1) the secured party's reasonable expenses of collecting and enforcing the agreement, including preparing and selling the collateral, and whatever the parties have agreed to for legal fees and expenses that is within the law;

(2) satisfying the obligations that were secured;

(3) satisfying obligations due a *subordinate* security interest or lien in the collateral, so long as:

(A) the foreclosing secured party receives an authenticated demand from the subordinate party before the proceeds have been completely distributed; and

(B) the subordinate security interest or lien is senior to the interest of a consignor. If it's not, then the consignor wins.

(4) a secured party that is a consignor if the foreclosing secured party receives an authenticated demand from the consignor before the proceeds have been completely distributed.

(b) A subordinate interest must provide reasonable proof of its interest or lien within a reasonable time after the priority security interest holder asks. Unless the request is complied with, the priority interest does not need to honor a demand under (a)(3).

(c) A secured party does not need to apply or pay over non-cash proceeds under **9–610** unless it would be commercially unreasonable not to. When it does apply them, the secured party must apply the proceeds in a commercially reasonable manner.

(d) If the security interest under which foreclosure and disposition is made secures payment or performance of an obligation, then after payments and applications required by (a) and permitted by (c):

(1) unless (a)(4) gives a consignor the right to payment of proceeds, the secured party must account to and pay the debtor any surplus generated from the disposition; and

(2) the obligor has to pay any deficiency.

(e) When you're dealing with a security interest arising from a sale of accounts, chattel paper, payment intangibles, or promissory notes, the debtor doesn't get any surplus and the obligor doesn't have to pay any deficiency.

(f) To calculate how much of a surplus or deficiency exists, figure out how much in proceeds would have been realized in a disposition that complied with the **9–600s** procedures to someone other than the secured party, a person related to the secured party or a secondary obligor (like a guarantor) if:

(1) the transferee of the collateral on disposition is one of those parties; and

(2) the proceeds received are significantly below the range you would expect if the **9–600s** were followed, and the disposition was to someone who is not one of those parties.

(g) A secured party that receives cash proceeds from a disposition in good faith and doesn't know that receipt violates the rights of another security interest or a lien that has priority over the lower-ranking security interest or agricultural lien:

(1) takes the cash proceeds free of the priority security interest or lien;

(2) doesn't need to apply the proceeds toward obligations secured by the priority interest or lien; and

(3) doesn't have to account to or pay the priority interest or lien for any surplus.

9–616: EXPLAINING HOW A SURPLUS OR DEFICIENCY IS CALCULATED

(a) In this section:

(1) "Explanation" means something in writing that:

(A) states the amount of the surplus or deficiency;

(B) explains under paragraph (c) how the secured party calculated the surplus or deficiency;

(C) if applicable, states that future charges or credits, and things like interest, expenses, etc., may affect the amount of surplus or deficiency; and

(D) gives a telephone number or mailing address from which to get additional information.

(2) "Request" means a record:

(A) authenticated by a debtor or consumer obligor;

(B) requesting that the recipient provide an explanation; and

(C) sent after disposition of the collateral under 9–610.

(b) In a consumer-goods transaction where the debtor is entitled to a surplus or a consumer obligor is liable for a deficiency under 9–615, the secured party must:

(1) send an explanation to the debtor or consumer obligor after the disposition:

(A) before or when the secured party pays a surplus or first makes a written demand for payment of a deficiency; and

(B) within 14 days after receipt of a request; or

(2) if it's a consumer obligor who is liable for a deficiency, waive its right to a deficiency in writing, within 14 days after receiving a "request".

(c) To comply with (a)(1)(B), the writing must have the following information in exactly this order:

(1) the lump sum of obligations that the security interest covered, and the amount of a rebate of unearned interest or credit service charge, if applicable, calculated as of a specific date:

(A) not more than 35 days before the secured party takes or receives possession of the collateral after default, if that's what it does; or

(B) not more than 35 days before the disposition if the secured party either receives possession *before* default or *doesn't* take possession at all;

(2) the amount of proceeds received from the disposition;

(3) the lump sum total of obligations left after deducting the amount of proceeds;

(4) the *amount*, in lump sum or broken out by type, and the *types* of expenses that may be recoverable under the security agreement and Article Nine, which relate to the disposition and which the secured party knows;

(5) the *amount*, in lump sum or broken out by type, and the *types* of credits to which the obligor is known to be entitled and which aren't covered in (c)(1); and

(6) the amount of the surplus or deficiency.

(d) There is no particular phrasing required for an explanation. An explanation that substantially complies with the requirements of (a) is sufficient, even if it has errors that aren't seriously misleading.

(e) A debtor or consumer obligor gets one free response to a request under this section once in each six-month period when the secured party didn't send them an explanation under (b)(1). The secured party may charge up to $25 for each additional response.

9–617: TRANSFEREE'S RIGHTS

(a) When a secured party disposes of collateral after default:

(1) a transferee for value gets all the debtor's rights in the collateral;

(2) the disposition discharges the foreclosing secured party's security interest; and

(3) the disposition discharges any subordinate security interest or lien [except for: list exceptions to this here, if any].

(b) A transferee that acts in good faith gets the benefits of (a) even if the secured party didn't comply with Article Nine or the specifics of a judicial ruling.

(c) If a transferee *doesn't* qualify for (a)'s benefits, then the collateral the transferee gets is subject to:

(1) the debtor's rights in the collateral as if those had not been transferred;

(2) the security interest or lien interest that made the disposition; and

(3) any other security interest or lien.

Note: Observe how these rules work with the other sections of Article Nine. If a junior secured party follows the 9–600s, it must provide any surplus from the collateral's disposition to help satisfy the rights of other secured parties and lien holders that are *junior* to the foreclosing secured party. But, the junior secured party need not provide any surplus to any *senior* secured parties or other interests. 9–615(g).

Where does that leave the senior interests? A senior security interest still has its 9–315 rights to follow the collateral wherever it goes, because nothing in these rules cuts off that right. For example, we're not talking about an ordinary course of business sale, which would cut off enforcement of the rights of a secured party in inventory. Instead, the foreclosing secured party's transferee in a foreclosure sale situation gets all of the original debtor's rights, but those rights include whatever limitations existed on them, including the now-continuing rights of the senior secured party. So, unless the junior, foreclosing secured party wants to deal with a very angry transferee that finds the senior secured party demanding return of the collateral, the junior party is well advised to consult with any senior interest before disposing of the collateral.

Notice further that 9–610(d) says that the disposition by the junior secured party includes warranties about things like good title, so the angry transferee will have excellent standing to go after the transferor. Although 9–610(e) allows the transferring junior secured party to disclaim these kinds of warranties, that's likely to be a red flag for any potential transferee.

9–618: SECONDARY OBLIGORS' RIGHTS AND OBLIGATIONS

(a) A secondary obligor, such as a guarantor, gets a secured party's rights and obligations if:

(1) they get an assignment of the security interest from the secured party;

(2) the secured party transfers the collateral to them and they agree to assume the secured party's position; or

(3) they are subrogated to the secured party's rights when it comes to the collateral.

(b) An assignment, transfer, or subrogation under (a) is not a "disposition" of collateral under 9–610, and it relieves the secured party of any further Article Nine duties.

9–619: TRANSFER STATEMENTS

(a) In this section, "transfer statement" means an authenticated record from a secured party that says:

(1) the debtor defaulted on an obligation secured by the collateral;

(2) the secured party foreclosed on the collateral;

(3) a transferee acquired the debtor's rights in the collateral by virtue of the foreclosure; and

(4) here are the secured party's, debtor's, and transferee's names and mailing addresses.

(b) Where the collateral is a kind that has a filing system covering its ownership, such as a certificate of title, copyright filing, etc., a transfer statement entitles the transferee to switch the registrations to itself. If a transfer statement is presented to the filing office with the appropriate fee and request form, the office must:

(1) accept the transfer statement;

(2) promptly amend its records to show the transfer; and

(3) issue a new certificate of title, if appropriate, to the transferee.

(c) A transfer to a secured party under (b) isn't itself a disposition of collateral under Article Nine and doesn't relieve the secured party of its Article Nine duties.

9–620: STRICT FORECLOSURE

(a) Except for (g), a secured party may accept collateral in full or partial satisfaction of the obligation it secures, without having to *sell* the collateral, only if:

(1) the debtor agrees under (c);

(2) the secured party doesn't receive in the time set out in (d) an objection authenticated by:

(A) someone to whom the secured party was required to send a proposal under 9–621; or

(B) anyone other than the debtor who has a subordinate interest in the collateral;

(3) the collateral is not in the debtor's possession when the debtor agrees, if you're dealing with consumer goods; and

(4) a secured party is not required to dispose of the collateral under (e), or the debtor waives that requirement under 9–624.

(b) Even if it seems the collateral has been accepted by the secured party, the so-called acceptance is not effective unless:

(1) the secured party consents in an authenticated record or sends a proposal to the debtor; and

(2) the requirements of (a) are met.

(c) For purposes of this section:

(1) A debtor consents to a *partial* satisfaction only if it agrees to the terms of acceptance by the secured party in a *post*-default authenticated record. A pre-default agreement doesn't count; and

(2) A debtor consents to a *full* satisfaction only by agreeing to the terms of a *post*-default authenticated record (again, a pre-default agreement doesn't count), or the secured party:

(A) sends the debtor a *post*-default proposal that is unconditioned or has only the condition that collateral not in the secured party's possession be preserved or maintained;

(B) agrees in the proposal to accept the collateral in full or partial satisfaction of the debt; and

(C) does not receive the debtor's authenticated notification of objection within 20 days after sending the proposal.

(d) To be effective under (a)(2), a secured party must receive a notice of objection:

(1) within 20 days after sending notice to a person who gets the notice under 9–621; and

(2) if (d)(1) doesn't apply:

(A) within 20 days after a 9–621 notification was sent; or

(B) before the debtor consents under (c) if no notification was sent.

(e) A secured party who takes possession must dispose of the collateral under the rules of 9–610 within the time set forth in (f) if:

(1) 60 percent of the cash price has been paid on a consumer goods purchase money security interest; or

(2) 60 percent of the principal amount owed on the secured debt has been paid on a non-purchase-money consumer goods debt.

(f) To comply with (e), the secured party must dispose of the collateral:

(1) within 90 days of taking possession; or

(2) within a longer period agreed to by the debtor and secondary obligor in an authenticated agreement *after* default. Pre-default agreements don't count.

(g) A secured party can't accept collateral in partial satisfaction of a debt in a consumer transaction. In other words, in a consumer transaction, if the secured party wants to get the goods as some kind of satisfaction of what's owed, it has to be a complete satisfaction, leaving no room for a deficiency claim.

9–621: NOTIFICATION OF STRICT FORECLOSURE

(a) A secured party seeking collateral in full or partial satisfaction of a debt must send its notice to:

(1) anyone from whom the secured party received, before the debtor's consent, an authenticated notice of a claim of interest in the collateral;

(2) any other secured party or lien holder that perfected its interest by filing at least 10 days before the debtor consented, if the filing:

(A) identified the collateral;

(B) was indexed under the debtor's name by that date; and

(C) was filed in the proper place by that date; and

(3) any other secured party that held an interest in the collateral perfected by compliance with a statute, regulation or treaty under 9–311(a) at least 10 days before the debtor consented.

(b) In addition to the parties covered in (a), the secured party must also send its notice to any secondary obligor.

9–622: EFFECT OF STRICT FORECLOSURE

(a) When a secured party accepts collateral in full or partial satisfaction of the debt it covers, this:

(1) discharges the debt to the extent the debtor agrees;

(2) gives the secured party all the debtor's rights in the collateral;

(3) discharges the security interest or agricultural lien that covered the collateral, even if the collateral's value doesn't cover all of the debt still owed under (a)(1), and discharges subordinate interests and liens; and

(4) negates any other subordinate interest.

(b) Even if the secured party didn't comply with Article Nine, subordinate interests are discharged or terminated under (a). However, those interests may go after the secured party under 9–625 for its failure to comply.

9–623: REDEMPTION OF COLLATERAL

(a) Anyone may redeem collateral, including the debtor, a secondary obligor or any other secured party or lien holder.

(b) To redeem collateral, you provide payment for:

(1) everything owed that was covered by the collateral; and

(2) the reasonable expenses and attorney's fees under 9–615(a)(1).

(c) Redemption may occur any time before a secured party:

(1) collects the collateral under 9–607;

(2) disposes of the collateral or contracts for disposition under 9–610; or

(3) accepts collateral in full or partial satisfaction of the debt under 9–622.

9–624: WHAT CAN BE WAIVED

(a) A debtor or secondary obligor may waive their right to be notified about a disposition under 9–611 only if they make a *post*-default authenticated agreement saying that.

(b) A debtor may only waive the right to the 9–620(e) mandatory disposition (the “60 percent” procedures) if they make an authenticated agreement saying that after default.

(c) Except for consumer-goods transactions, which may have different rules under state and federal law, a debtor or secondary obligor may waive their right to redeem collateral under 9–623 only if they make a *post*-default authenticated agreement saying that.

9–625: WHEN THE SECURED PARTY FAILS TO COMPLY

(a) Courts may enter into the secured party's efforts at foreclosure, disposition, etc., if it's shown those efforts aren't proceeding properly under Article Nine.

(b) Except for (c), (d), and (f), a person must pay damages for their failure to comply with Article Nine. If the failure to comply harms the debtor's ability to get alternative financing, that can be part of the damages paid.

(c) Except for 9–628:

(1) Whoever was a debtor, obligor, secured party, or lien-holder in the collateral at the time of a failure to comply with Article Nine may recover damages under (b); and

(2) If the collateral is consumer goods and the secured party fails to follow the rules in the 9–600s, anyone who is a debtor or secondary obligor at the time of the failure automatically gets damages at least in the amount of the credit service charge plus 10 percent of the principal amount owed, or at least the time value of the amount owed plus 10 percent of the cash price. In most cases, the credit service charge will be the interest charge.

(d) If 9–626 voids a debtor's deficiency, the debtor may get paid for its loss of surplus on a disposition of the collateral. But if a debtor's or secondary obligor's deficiency is eliminated or reduced by 9–626, they can't also recover under (b) for noncompliance with Article Nine.

(e) A debtor, consumer obligor or person named as a debtor in a filing gets $500 in each case in addition to any other damages from a person that:

(1) doesn't comply with 9–208;

(2) doesn't comply with 9–209;

(3) files a record they're not entitled to under 9–509(a);

(4) doesn't cause a secured party of record to file or send a termination statement as required in 9–513(a) or (c);

(5) has a pattern or consistent habit of not complying with 9–616(b)(1); or

(6) doesn't comply with 9–616(b)(2).

(f) A debtor or consumer obligor may get damages under (b) plus $500 from someone who fails to comply with a request under 9–210 without reasonable cause. If someone receives a request under 9–210 but never claimed an interest in the collateral or the obligations covered, then they have a reasonable excuse for failing to comply with the request.

(g) If a secured party fails to comply with a 9–210 request to provide a list of collateral or a statement of account, then as against a person misled by the failure, they may claim a security interest only to the extent of what is shown in the list or statement that came with the request.

9–626: RULES IF AN ISSUE ABOUT DEFICIENCY OR SURPLUS EXISTS

(a) In transactions other than consumer ones, use these rules if there is an issue about deficiency or surplus:

(1) A secured party doesn't have to prove it complied with the 9–600s on collection, enforcement disposition or acceptance unless the debtor or a secondary obligor puts it in issue.

(2) If the secured party's compliance is put in issue, the secured party has the burden of proving it complied with the 9–600s.

(3) Except for 9–628, if a secured party fails to prove it complied with the 9–600s, a debtor's or secondary obligor's liability for deficiency is limited as follows: add the secured obligation, expenses, and attorney's fees together, and see if that sum is more than the greater of the following:

(A) the proceeds of collection, enforcement, disposition, or acceptance; or

(B) the amount of proceeds that would have been obtained if the secured party had followed the 9–600 rules.

The deficiency liability is only the excess of the obligation and expense sum over either (A) or (B), whichever applies.

(4) For (3)(B), the amount of proceeds that would have been realized is the sum of the secured obligation, expenses, and attorney's fees, unless the secured party proves it's less. This means the rebuttable presumption against a secured party that doesn't follow the rules is that if the rules *had* been followed there would be no deficiency.

(5) If deficiency or surplus is calculated under 9–615(f), it's the debtor's or obligor's burden to prove that the proceeds received are significantly below the range of prices that a proper disposition to a true third party would have brought.

(b) The reason (a) applies to *non*-consumer transactions is so the courts can determine the rules to apply in consumer cases. A court should not use (a) to fashion new rules for consumer cases, but may continue to apply established approaches for those cases.

9–627: WHEN IS CONDUCT COMMERCIALLY REASONABLE?

(a) Just because the secured party might have obtained a greater amount by a collection, enforcement, disposition, or acceptance with a different time or method doesn't stop the secured party from showing what it actually did was commercially reasonable.

(b) A disposition of collateral is commercially reasonable if it's made:

(1) in the usual way on a recognized market;

(2) at the then-current price on a recognized market; or

(3) in conformity with reasonable commercial practices by dealers in the same type of property.

(c) A collection, enforcement, disposition, or acceptance is commercially reasonable if it is approved:

(1) by a court;

(2) by a bona fide creditors' committee;

(3) by a representative of creditors; or

(4) by an assignee for the benefit of creditors.

(d) The approvals in (c) don't need to be obtained, and lack of approval doesn't mean a secured party's action was not commercially reasonable.

9–628: LIMITATIONS ON SECURED PARTY'S LIABILITY

(a) Unless a secured party knows a person is a debtor or obligor and knows how to communicate with them:

(1) the secured party is not liable to them or to a secured party or lien holder that filed a financing statement, for failure to comply with Article Nine; and

(2) the secured party's failure to comply with Article Nine doesn't affect the person's liability for a deficiency.

(b) A secured party is not automatically liable:

(1) to a debtor or obligor unless the secured party knows:

(A) that's what they are;

(B) their identity; and

(C) how to communicate with them; or

(2) to a secured party or lien holder that filed a financing statement against a person, unless the secured party knows:

(A) that the person is a debtor; and

(B) their identity.

(c) A secured party won't be held liable for, and any deficiency claim is not affected by, an act or omission if the secured party reasonably believed the transaction isn't a consumer-goods or consumer transaction or that goods are not consumer goods, if it reasonably relied on:

(1) what the debtor told it; or

(2) what an obligor told it about why the secured obligation was being incurred.

(d) A secured party is not liable to anyone under 9–625(c)(2) for failing to comply with 9–616.

(e) A secured party is not liable under 9–625(c)(2) more than once on a single secured obligation.